Maeve de Markievicz:

Daughter of Constance

Clive Scoular

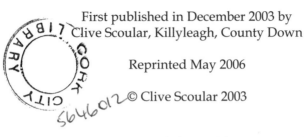

First published in December 2003 by
Clive Scoular, Killyleagh, County Down

Reprinted May 2006

© Clive Scoular 2003

ISBN 0-9539601-2-9

Photograph Acknowledgements

The author wishes to thank the following for permission to use photographs;
Messrs Weidenfeld and Nicolson, printers of Anne Marreco's book 'The Rebel Countess: the Life and Times of Constance Markievicz' for those on pages 15, 21, 38 and 40.
Mrs B. Wells, page 52.
Mrs M James, page 52.
Mrs Rita Lees, page 69.
Mr Joe McGowan for his agreement to use two photographs on pages 28 and 35.
Mr Edward Walsh, Contents page
The remainder of the photographs are the work of the author himself.

Printed in Northern Ireland by
W & G Baird Limited
Caulside Drive
Antrim
Northern Ireland
BT41 2RS

For Thomas -

just exceptional

Contents

Foreword

I met Maeve Markievicz when she came to Ireland for her first exhibition of her paintings.

She was a tall, strikingly handsome, woman not of the classical beauty of her mother but with the same fine bone structure. Her mother, Constance, had that air of breeding which allowed her to walk with kings whilst Maeve had the common touch which enabled her to mix with the farm workers of Lissadell.

She had immediate empathy with everyone she met, both great and small. Nor did she suffer fools gladly as I soon discovered in a letter which she had written to me concerning a painting of the church in Collooney I had asked her to paint. The following is an extract from that letter.

'Your name is mud - the girl who so kindly took the picture over for me has kept on asking me whether it arrived and I had to say that you could not be bothered to acknowledge it - even after a postcard and a letter from me'. Maeve ended the letter - 'In haste for post as I like to acknowledge things by return!'

She also told me that on her visit to Ireland she had met a prominent businessman who had said - 'I was madly in love with you when I was a young man' - to which she replied - 'Why did you not tell me? - to which he replied - 'I thought you were not attainable by me' - to which she retorted - 'Nonsense'.

I know, too, that one day an official lunch was being given for her as the guest of honour in a Sligo hotel when, before entering the dining room, she asked to see a young man, a native of Lissadell, who was working in the kitchens. She wanted to give him a message from his mother. When he was sent up to see Maeve she gave him the letter together with a gift of money. Only then did she proceed to her place at the top table.

In her last letter to me less than two weeks before her death, Maeve said she wanted to paint a picture for me. Unfortunately this was not to be. Death intervened. May she rest in peace.

Jim McGarry
Collooney
County Sligo
October 2003

Introduction

In recent times when I have been giving talks about Constance, the question was often asked of me 'Whatever happened to Maeve?' My answer was simple. I knew nothing of her life, so I decided to undertake some research and to write this book

The life of Maeve Markievicz is an unremarkable one. She lived a secluded and, in many ways, an uneventful life at the home of her grandmother and in a number of homes in England. It often appeared that she left Ireland to exorcise the memory of her famous - or infamous - mother, Constance. She did, however, return to Ireland in the last days of her life where she rekindled the love of her own country which she had done so much to extinguish in her early life. Although she qualified as a landscape gardener and was most proficient in her occupation, she reverted to family type and became a painter in her later life.

Maeve spent well over a decade living in the quiet village of Egerton in the tranquil Kent countryside and it is there that she is still remembered. The villagers loved the eccentric and kindly lady whom they knew to have had a remarkable mother. They were sad to take leave of her as World War Two broke out.

Maeve Markievicz is certainly not noteworthy as a political figure nor does she even reach the lower ranks of Irish historical importance, but she does warrant a place in the story of Ireland as the one and only child of one of Ireland's foremost, and sadly often forgotten, Irish heroines, Constance Markievicz. Her biography helps to complete the jigsaw of the women of 20th century Ireland.

I wish to express my thanks to all those who helped me in my research and I particularly want to mention the people of Egerton who held Maeve Markievicz in such high esteem and also the late Jim McGarry of Collooney, county Sligo, who not only shared his memories of Maeve but also agreed to write the foreword to the book. I appreciate the help given by the new owner of Lissadell, Edward Walsh, whose commitment to the Markievicz legacy will ensure that the house and its history will not be forgotten.

Clive Scoular
Killyleagh
May 2006

Gore-Booth Family Tree

1842-2003

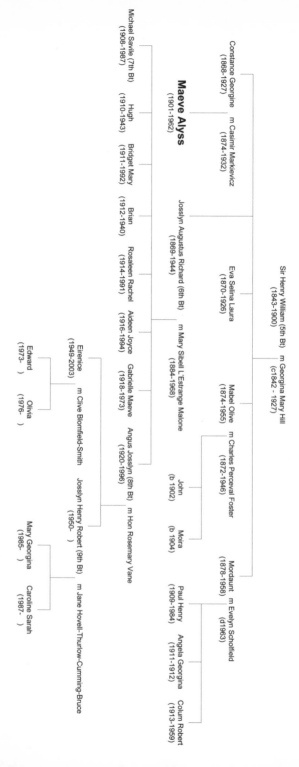

1

A Birth at Lissadell

County Sligo, in the west of Ireland, is an area of exceptional and outstanding beauty with its extensive woods, its sandy beaches and its shimmering vistas. Situated north of the town of Sligo and near to the village of Drumcliffe, made famous by the poet William B. Yeats, lies the Lissadell estate, home of the Gore-Booth family since the creation of the baronetcy in 1760. The family seat is one of Ireland's finest Big Houses – a square, gaunt, limestone, neo-classical house standing amongst high trees at the end of a long and winding driveway.

This particular house, built between 1830 and 1837, replaced another mansion which had stood nearer the sea. Hidden from the public gaze and the prying eye, it completely surprises and beguiles the unsuspecting visitor as he approaches the imposing stately home. Surrounding Lissadell stand two fine and majestic mountains. Knocknarea towers almost 2,000 feet over Sligo Bay to the south and, according to Irish folklore, is the burial place of the legendary Queen Maeve. Benbulben – a bare, flat-topped mountain to the north east – is less imposing than Knocknarea and somewhat sullenly overlooks the family estate.

Here at Lissadell, in the early hours of Thursday 13 November 1901, a child was born. Hers was not an easy delivery for a 30-something first time mother. However, with the skill of an eminent gynaecologist and the family doctor, little Maeve Alyss made her appearance. Her mother was exhausted and yet relieved; her father stood tall. Maeve was the latest member of the Gore-Booth family although this was not her surname. She had an unusual last name, one which was to become synonymous with the struggle for Irish independence within a few short years following her birth. She was a Markievicz, the daughter of Constance Gore-Booth and Casimir Dunin de Markievicz, a minor Polish nobleman from far-off Zyvotov in Poland (in the modern day Ukraine). Her parents had chosen for the confinement to take place in Ireland where they knew they could

Lissadell

count on excellent medical attention. Since the child's birth turned out to be a particularly difficult one, they had chosen wisely. Immediately after her birth, the little child was whisked off to be cared for by the family nurses and faithful retainers. Despite the circumstances of her birth, Maeve grew into a strong and lively baby.

The story is told that, upon arrival at Lissadell at the end of October, the heavily pregnant Constance disobeyed her doctor's orders and chose to participate in a riding expedition. 'Leaving the avenue, Madame (Constance) led the party cross country. In a pasture field the Lissadell cows were lying chewing their cuds. An irresponsible member of the party dared Madame to jump her mount across one of the cows. Accepting the challenge without hesitation, she drove her mount at the nearest cow. Just as she approached, the cow stood up. Madame spurred forward and to the horror of the others jumped across the bewildered cow.'[1] Upon hearing this story later in life, Maeve was to remark 'Is it any wonder that I am not beautiful?.'

Many people asked why the child had been given the names Maeve and Alyss. The answer is a combination of speculation and fact. During her childhood, Constance had often looked over Drumcliffe Bay and gazed upon the mountain where the warrior Queen Maeve's burial mound stands. She loved stories of Irish folklore and it seemed perfectly natural for any daughter of hers to be given that magical name. 'Now, in memory of the ancient Gaelic heroine for whom a cairn stands on Knocknarea's summit, the daughter whose birth nearly caused her mother's death was christened Maeve'. [2] This is the speculation.

The fact of the matter is that the child's second name, Alyss, (Irish for Alice) was almost certainly given as a reminder of a beautiful girl with whom Casimir (always Casi to the family) had fallen in love when he was in Paris whilst he was also courting Constance. This Alyss had even given Casi a ring as a token of her love for him even though she knew that he had chosen to marry Constance and not her. It seems quite bizarre that Constance should have agreed to this name as it would have been

Benbulben

11

a constant reminder to both of them of the affection between Alyss and Casi. Yet it shows the unconventional nature of Constance in deciding to perpetuate the memory of the 'other woman' in an amorous triangle by giving her daughter this name.

And, in Dublin at that very time, the Markieviczs' friend, the playwright Edward Martyn, had his play 'Alyss' on stage and this confirmed Constance in the choice of this other very Irish name for her daughter.

The Christmas season at Lissadell was, as in all the Big Houses in Ireland, a time for family reunion. There was much seasonal jollity with staff working harder than ever to provide sumptuous meals for the squire, his family and his guests. But there had been significant recent changes at Lissadell. The much loved 5th baronet, Sir Henry, had died at the relatively young age of 56 just two years previously in January 1900 and his elder son, Sir Josslyn, the uncle of the newborn infant, was the new master of Lissadell. He was, at Christmas 1901, 32 years old and as yet unmarried. His mother, Lady Gore-Booth, was therefore no longer mistress and was preparing to move out of the Big House to make way for her son as she did not want to be there when her son found himself a wife.

When Sir Josslyn did marry in June 1907 Lady Gore-Booth moved to a house at Ballytivnan, near Sligo, and then to a smaller dower house called 'Ardeevin', eight miles from Lissadell on the road from Sligo to Rosses Point. This house was far enough away to allow her son the rights and privileges of his new position, but close enough to give help and advice – and motherly care – as and when the need arose.

Sir Henry had been an avid Arctic explorer which, in the latter part of the nineteenth century, was a bold and exciting vocation. He had sailed several times almost as far as the Arctic Circle which was no mean feat for an intrepid gentleman of a Big House. He had even taken his faithful butler, Kilgallon, on one of these expeditions during which he had actually saved his master's life by shooting a huge bear that was about to devour Sir Henry. Various Arctic memorabilia, such as the stuffed bear, walrus tusks, a whale's skull and assorted birds and fish are still very much in evidence at Lissadell to this day. There is, deep in the Arctic Ocean, Gore-Booth Island named in memory of the gallant Sir Henry. Lady Gore-Booth had been a most long-suffering woman to have been able to cope with her growing family whilst the master of the house was absent on his frequent, lengthy and dangerous voyages.

And now it was Sir Josslyn who sat at the head of the table at the festive activities at Lissadell that Christmas of 1901. Completing the immediate Gore-Booth family circle were his mother, his sisters Constance, Eva and Mabel and his younger brother, Mordaunt. Also present were Constance's husband, Casi, and their newborn daughter close by in the nursery.

A controversial choice

The only one of the late Sir Henry's children who was married at that time was Constance. Her marriage the previous year to her impecunious Polish nobleman had caused some raising of eyebrows, not only within the immediate family circle, but also amongst many of the other landed families of Ireland. Constance, however, had always been an eccentric and self-willed child who, although presented at the court of Queen Victoria during the sovereign's golden jubilee year in 1887, had never conformed to the norms expected of a gentry daughter.

She had always been hugely popular with the eligible young gentlemen from the ranks of the nobility and from many well-to-do families who had endeavoured, but failed, to sweep Constance off her feet. She evidently had a mind of her own and, by the mid 1890s, she had persuaded her parents to permit her to go to study art, firstly at the Slade in London, and then at the world renowned Julian's studio in Paris. Her parents' fervent wish to mould their rebellious daughter had been singularly unsuccessful and, although they had reduced her allowance considerably in an attempt to bring her to heel, Constance's independent streak and stubbornness enabled her to live, comfortably enough, on the very meagre amount of two French francs a day.

While she was in Paris, Constance's father and mother had travelled to Switzerland, to the fashionable resort of St Moritz, to seek a cure for Sir Henry's ailments. But this visit was to no avail, for it was there, on 13 January 1900, that Sir Henry died. The family, particularly Lady Gore-Booth and Constance, was devastated and heartbroken. They returned to Lissadell for the respectful period of mourning. In due course, Constance moved back to Paris to continue her studies – and also to pursue her Casimir.

Prior to Sir Henry's death, he and his wife had discussed their daughter's future. The fact that Constance had fallen for an impoverished foreign nobleman – and a Roman Catholic widower with a three year old son to boot – clearly caused some Gore-Booth heart-searching. In fact, so concerned were they about their daughter's choice of husband, that they had arranged through the British ambassador in St Petersburg to have a spy from the Russian Secret Service investigate Casimir whilst he was in Paris. Nothing particularly untoward was uncovered and, in the end, they had given their rather reluctant approval to their nuptials.

They realised that their eldest daughter would simply marry Casimir Markievicz anyway, so they considered it politic that they should approve. Constance was, nonetheless, happy that she had her parents' blessing for her marriage and she was also even old-fashioned enough to encourage Casimir to seek the Gore-Booth seal of approval by asking her father for her hand in marriage. But when Sir Henry died, their marriage plans had to be put on hold. However before long, the family agreed that the wedding should go ahead, although with less flourish than would otherwise have been the case.

A London wedding

The wedding took place at St Mary's Parish Church in Marylebone in London on 29 September 1900. The Church of England was chosen, being the Anglican sister church of Constance's childhood Church of Ireland. A great family friend, the Reverend Frederick Sheridan Le Fanu, the rector at Lissadell, travelled to the capital to officiate at the church wedding. Constance had her two sisters, Eva and Mabel, and two of her friends, Rachel Mansfield and Mildred Grenfell, as her only bridesmaids. Had her father still been alive, she would have had at least eight attendants, various page boys and flower girls – and a long flowing train as would have befitted any daughter of the local baronet. There were two other wedding ceremonies that day, one at the local registry office and another at the Russian legation. Constance and Casimir spent their honeymoon travelling throughout parts of northern France on their new bicycles.

Later in the year, Constance travelled with Casi to his home in the Ukraine where she met her husband's family for the first time. She was an immediate hit with them and their retainers. She impressed them all as a feisty and remarkable lady – who certainly did not appear to them to be the archetypal daughter who had been brought up on a great Irish

Constance and Casimir on their wedding day, 29 September 1900

estate. There, in a little studio specially prepared for them, Constance and Casimir pursued their painting careers.

It was during this visit that Constance first met her stepson, the four year old Stanislaus. He was the son of her husband by his first wife, the young and beautiful Jadwiga, who had died in Paris, along with her younger son, Ryszard, two years before Casi had met Constance. In later years Stanislaus was to recall his first meeting with his stepmother and her initial impressions of him. 'We took to each other at once. She was, in my childish eyes, like a goddess from another world, and her heart went out to the winsome and rather lonely child with the big pathetic eyes and curly golden hair'.[3]

Soon after Maeve's birth, around Christmas 1901, a date was arranged for Maeve to be christened. For years Gore-Booths had been baptised at Lissadell Parish Church by their own local rector. Lissadell church (or Ballinful, as the locals call it) lies outside the main estate grounds.

Lissadell Parish Church

For an estate church, the building is remarkably large and imposing. Standing as it does amongst high trees and rather hidden from the road in the summer months, the church has a high pointed tower with a clock, presented by the grateful tenantry in memory of Sir Robert Gore-Booth, and a lofty roof.

Inside the building the atmosphere was somewhat grave and dank. But in 1907 two incredibly beautiful, distinctive and exquisite east windows -'Harmonia' and 'Fortitudo', were dedicated in memory of Augusta Gore-Booth – the family's beloved 'Wee Ga', who played the church organ for many years. These windows were attributed to Sarah Purser's talented pupil, Ethel Rhind, and made at 'An Tur Gloine' – the Tower of Glass in Dublin.* A small two-manual, hand-bellowed, organ in a fine mahogany case, is situated below the sanctuary steps.

There are over three hundred seats in the church, including a north aisle extension built in the late 1800s to accommodate the large numbers of parishioners who attended Sunday services, mainly estate workers and

*After the end of World War Two, two further windows, designed by another of 'An Tur Gloine's' artists, Kitty O'Brien, were presented by Mary, Lady Gore-Booth, in memory of two of her sons, Hugh and Brian, who were lost in action during the war.

their families. A little brass plaque near the chancel steps records the fact that 'the foundation stone of this church was laid on the 17th day of June 1856 by Hannah, Lady Gore-Booth'.

Lissadell church, even with its extension, still proved to be too small for the congregation and St Kevin's chapel of ease was built in 1896 at Munninane, about two miles distant, 'motivated by Lissadell rector Frederick Sheridan Le Fanu because too many parishioners at that end of the parish were attending the new gospel hall that George Siggins had built across the road from his house at Cashelgarron, and so Munninane was built to try and get them back – very successfully it would seem, judging by its swelling and loyal population today'.[4]

The baptismal roll at Lissadell recalls the acceptance of little Maeve into the fold of the Church of Ireland on Sunday 11 January 1902. The Reverend Frederick S. Le Fanu christened the child although he did make a number of errors in the information entered in the baptismal register. Maeve's date of birth was given as 14 November 1901 and her father's name was given as 'Cassimir de Markie'. Clearly the rector had been rather casual when recording the birth by allowing these inaccuracies to appear on such an important document.

Even though the baptism took place on a cold January day, the church was filled with godparents and family members, amidst an adoring congregation of estate workers and household staff. In those days it was customary for the family retainers to celebrate the birth of a child to their employer, but this state of affairs was very quickly to change throughout Ireland as Big House staff soon turned their faces against their employers and engaged in violent and murderous attacks on their landlords during the 1919-1921 War of Independence. Although Lissadell was largely spared from these attacks, possibly because of Constance's connections with the republican cause, there was at least one isolated raid on the house in search of arms in 1920.

Carriages brought the guests from the church immediately following the service and a special meal was served in the grand dining room to celebrate the day's event. But life was quickly to change at Lissadell for Maeve when her mother abandoned her in order to pursue a very different life-style – and one certainly not associated with the ladies of the Big House.

2

Maeve's Early Years at Lissadell

After a few days the family dispersed. Lady Gore-Booth remained at Lissadell, whilst Constance's two sisters went back to their homes in England - Eva to Manchester where she pursued her social work vocation in the slums of that great city and Mabel to the south with her new husband, Perceval Foster. Neither was it long before Constance and Casi yearned to go back to their painting studio in Paris. They now had to consider what arrangements they should make for Maeve. She could, of course, be taken back to their decidedly spartan accommodation in the French capital unless some more suitable alternative scheme could be thought out for her.

It was decided that she would be left in the care of her grandmother. As it transpired, the young couple spent only a short time back in Paris, before revisiting Casi's family in the Ukraine. This was to be Constance's last visit to the home of her in-laws. They eventually returned to Dublin in 1903.

Back at Lissadell Maeve lived a lonely life. She was the only child in that great house amongst so many adults. Despite these circumstances she later realised that her happiest memories had originated from this period of her life. Along with her grandmother and her uncle, there were the house staff. Kilgallon, the butler who had explored the Arctic with the late Sir Henry, proved to be a wonderful companion for this spirited little girl and, along with the other under butlers, he made a great deal of fun for her.

The house was often full of dinner guests including, in the early days of the century, her own parents, Constance and Casimir. There were regular glittering balls at Lissadell at Christmas time and, although Maeve had been sent off early to bed on these occasions, she enjoyed sneaking out of her top floor nursery to spy upon the guests in the Great Hall below. Sometimes she even went down into the Hall and hid behind the curtains to watch the guests assembling. Just when Maeve thought that everyone had gone in to the ballroom, she heard a latecomer coming down the staircase singing off key as she made her entrance. As she peered out from her hiding place, Maeve saw that it was her own mother descending dressed in a wonderful, shimmering ball gown. As Maeve jumped out to greet her mother, Constance feigned annoyance by mildly chastising her daughter - 'You little devil, you've stolen the show!' The contrast between this beautiful apparition and the dreadful out of key singing had clearly greatly irritated the young child as she countered with her own rebuke - 'Why must she make that noise? Why can't she be content just to be beautiful?'[1]

But Maeve had another great delight as a youngster at Lissadell. She loved to twist Kilgallon and his under butlers and footmen around her little finger. She liked to think of these men as her staff slaves. They did not mind what Miss Maeve thought for they enjoyed her innocent pranks as well. She liked to play football in the top corridor where her room was situated. Kilgallon and the first footman would kick football with Maeve whilst the second footman stood guard at the top of the stairs.

On one occasion when a ball was going on in the house, Maeve had refused to go to bed until these men promised to come up later to play a game with her...

She could not contain herself in bed. After a while she got up and sat on the top step of the stairs, waiting. It seemed a long time for a child, before the ladies withdrew to the drawing room and the men got going on the port, for not until then would the butler be free. Just as she was beginning to nod, she saw a strange procession form at the bottom of the stairs. It was led by the first footman carrying a large silver salver with an equally large silver cover on it, who, in turn, was followed by the lordly butler carrying something too small to see on a cushion. Slowly and majestically they mounted the stairs until they reached the small girl in pigtails and long nightdress dancing excitedly on the landing. There they came to a halt. The butler bowed to the small child and offered her a silver whistle lying on the small cushion which she grabbed and had to be restrained from blowing immediately. But the time was not yet ripe for that. Then the second footman removed the cover from the salver to reveal a shining black topper underneath. The butler took the topper and carried it halfway down the corridor where he placed it on the floor. The second footman took up his position at the top of the stairs while the first footman and the butler took up theirs at either end of the corridor. The butler gave the signal. The small girl blew an ear-splitting whistle, kicked the topper in the direction of the butler and the game was on. It continued until the butler and the footman began to wilt and the small girl in the long nightdress and pigtails was sitting on the floor, the whistle still in her mouth, but too tired to blow it. And the topper was a topper no more![2]

And this accommodating Kilgallon was the one and the same butler whose larger-than-life portrait, painted by Casimir Markievicz, adorns the walls of the dining room at Lissadell to this very day. This fantastic story is simply an example of the fun which Maeve had in those happy days at Lissadell before she moved to Ardeevin with her grandmother.

Moving to Dublin: then to Ardeevin

Constance and Casi's first home, bought for them as a wedding present by Lady Gore-Booth, was in Dublin at St Mary's, Frankfort Avenue in the fashionable suburb of Rathgar. Maeve came up to stay with her parents shortly after they arrived back in Dublin. By now, and much to Constance's delight, Stanislaus (Staskou to the family) had arrived in Dublin from his grandmother's home in the Ukraine. His grandmother had been reluctant to part with her favourite grandchild but had eventually agreed that he should be with his father in Dublin. Staskou was excited at the prospect of travelling across half of Europe to his new home. 'All this was too much for my juvenile imagination and I treated the parting [from his grandmother] with cheerful nonchalance'.[3]

The Markievicz family was, for the first, and really the only time, complete and united. As parents, however, Constance and Casi left much to be desired preferring instead their life on the social round. Nonetheless Maeve and Staskou experienced happy days and enjoyed each other's company although Constance was a scatter-brained mother, with a slapdash attitude to child care. She once 'put the children into an apple tree to shake the fruit down and cared little that her daughter's dress was ruined in the branches'.[4] However, the children, according to Staskou, remember Constance as 'a tall, slim exquisite creature, clad in neat artist's overalls, with a crown of soft wavy golden-brown hair…with an indefinable faint scent - a mixture of some delicate perfume, paints and cigarettes'.[5]

For Constance and Casi life was hectic and unconventional. There were painting exhibitions to be mounted for they were both by now making names for themselves as proficient and talented artists. There were balls

Constance, Maeve and Staskou

to be attended at the Viceregal Lodge where it was 'de rigueur' to invite such fashionable guests as Casimir and Constance Markievicz. There were plays, many of them written by Casi himself, to be performed on the stage at the Abbey Theatre and in which Constance often acted, sometimes in a leading role, 'although she could not make her own personality subservient to the part she had to play'.[6]

This was hardly a suitable place for Maeve, although she did have faithful servants and nannies to care for her. By 1908, when she was just over six years old, the momentous decision was made to return Maeve permanently to her grandmother at Ardeevin. The die was cast - Maeve had now been banished from her own parental home. She would never again live, with any permanence, with Constance and Casi.

There were, of course, conflicting attitudes about leaving Maeve with Lady Gore-Booth. Maud Gonne was on the side of Constance for she considered it a great sacrifice for Constance to give up her daughter. 'I have heard people criticise Con for this and speak of her as being a neglectful mother. Nothing could be falser than that, but she was so unselfish she sacrificed everything for Ireland, and in this case did what she thought best for the child'.[7] Others, however, called Constance irresponsible for deserting her only child. 'That she may have wounded Maeve through an apparent coldness was to distress Constance later and she often sought to justify the child's country upbringing to women friends'.[8]

Constance, in truth, really liked boys better than girls; 'Madame had a way with boys. There was something in their own nature, free, imaginative, boisterous, indifferent to furniture, to which they responded. She was always more successful with boys than with girls and this led her to make her single most important contribution to Ireland, Fianna na hEireann'.[9]

It is hardly surprising that Maeve would now be, to all intents and purposes, abandoned. Even the favoured Staskou, although still a delicate boy and unhappy at the prospect, had been sent off to boarding school at Mount St. Benedict's in Gorey, county Wexford, in 1907. It almost seemed as if Constance had discarded her children rather as a spoiled child would have cast aside a rag doll or a much loved toy. It was time for her to grow up and growing up meant having no encumbrances to hinder her progress.

This year, 1908, was a watershed for the two emotionally deprived children. This was the time when they both realised that they would have to make their own way in the world without the steady and attentive love and care of parents. Constance and Casimir were too engrossed in their own self-centred pursuits to be troubled with their children. Little wonder that life for both Maeve and Staskou would end so unhappily.

Total commitment to the nationalist cause

By now Constance was 40 years old and had become energetically immersed in her new found activities. She had entered the sphere of nationalist politics and had made the acquaintance of Arthur Griffith, the founder of Sinn Fein. However he did not trust Constance, and he was never to waiver from this view. For her part, she admired Griffith although she did not trust him either. For a woman to enter politics was almost unheard of; for a daughter of the Big House to get involved in nationalist politics was unthinkable.

But Constance had made up her mind and she joined every organisation which would fulfil her ideals of a nationalist Ireland. Her early days in 'Inghinidhe na Eireann', the Daughters of Erin, had some comical interludes. Arriving for probably her first meeting in a cold, miserable and damp inner city Dublin hall, she entered with a flourish dressed in a fine evening gown and dripping with jewels. She had come to the meeting direct from a Viceregal function at Dublin Castle and she did not seem to notice the sour looks which were being cast her way by the more drably dressed women who were already there huddled around an open fire. This did not faze Constance as she proceeded to dry her wet boots by the fire and sit down to join in the proceedings.

She continued to become totally involved in every organisation that she joined. She became a member of the Gaelic League, although she could not be bothered to master the Irish language after many attempts to do so. She did, however, always support their events.

Her greatest triumph, undoubtedly, was the founding of the Fianna na hEireann who were her own brand of Boy Scouts firmly opposed to the ideals of Baden Powell's Boy Scout Movement which was beginning to expand throughout the world, including Ireland. Constance would have nothing to do with what she considered such a tame organisation for boys. Her boys would learn to shoot and drill rather than simply undertaking the more conventional Scouting activities like cooking and tying knots. And her Movement was to become the ideal recruiting ground for young men interested in pursuing an Ireland free from the Imperial yoke as well as an organisation which was to become infiltrated by members of the secret oath-bound Irish Republican Brotherhood (IRB). Fianna na hEireann produced many martyrs in the Irish cause, such as Liam Mellows, Con Colbert and Sean Heuston.

Maeve's life at Ardeevin

Maeve now permanently settled with her beloved grandmother, Gaga, at Ardeevin. Her mother's name was rarely mentioned either there or at Lissadell and Maeve herself found it increasingly difficult to think other than ill of her eccentric and distant mother. Her father, too, had become a mere shadow in the Dublin background. He was too interested in his writing, acting and painting careers to be concerned with his daughter.

However, for a number of years, at least until 1913, Constance and Casi did descend upon Lissadell for Christmas to join in the family festivities and there they were joined by Maeve and her grandmother from Ardeevin. But soon even this tenuous contact was to be severed. Maeve had to rely on her grandmother and her uncles and aunts to act as surrogate parents. She had to be content with this arrangement for there was no alternative. After the birth of the first of her cousins who lived at Lissadell - the children of her uncle Josslyn - Maeve did have some company, although these cousins were many years her junior.

Ardeevin, Maeve's childhood home

3

Maeve's Lonely Childhood

The year 1908 marked the beginning of what was to become, for Maeve, an essentially lonesome childhood. She was living at Ardeevin with her grandmother and, apart from Lady Gore-Booth's staff, Maeve was on her own. During these years her great aunt Madeline Wynne also came to stay.

Her uncle Josslyn, who had been master at Lissadell for seven years by this time, had finally married. He had taken as his bride his second cousin, Mary Sibell L'Estrange Malone, whose father was the Church of England vicar of Dalton Holme in Yorkshire (their grandmothers, Charlotte and Henrietta Lumley, had been sisters). Sir Josslyn was 38 and Mary 23 when the wedding took place on 12 June 1907. Lady Gore-Booth was doubtless relieved that her elder son had at last married thereby dispelling her fears that the heir to Lissadell would remain a bachelor.

Mary (or Molly, as the close members of the family always called her) was an affectionate young woman who had spent some of her holidays at Lissadell as a child and it was during her childhood years that she had become infatuated with her older cousin, Josslyn, although he was himself a somewhat reserved and withdrawn individual. She had 'hung her hat' at Josslyn and they entered upon their married life together full of hope and expectation. They were to be blessed with eight children, although there was to be much sadness and disappointment in the lives of their four sons and four daughters.

By the time that Sir Josslyn's first child, Michael, was born in July 1908, Maeve was almost seven years old. His birth was followed, in quick succession, by Hugh, born in June 1910, Bridget, in July 1911, Brian, in December 1912, Rosaleen, in August 1914, Aideen, in July 1916, Gabrielle, in August 1918 and finally by Angus, in June 1920. These children were greatly loved by Maeve, but she was always their much older cousin and not exactly their contemporary and bosom playmate. According to one of her cousins, Bridget, the very good looking Maeve was 'always unmerciful to us children and, in a sense, a bully who never knew when to stop. She also had a very loud masterful voice'.[1]

To complete the cousins on the Gore-Booth side, there were the two children of her Aunt Mabel and Uncle Percy, John and Moira, who were around the same age as Maeve, and the two surviving children of her uncle Mordaunt, Paul and Colum, who were born in 1909 and 1913 respectively. Their sister, Angela, had tragically died from whooping cough on New Year's Day 1912. Maeve enjoyed their company too although she only saw these cousins when they came over from their homes in England at holiday periods.

Later in life Maeve was to become very close to Colum. He had been an artistic and somewhat rebellious young man yet he and Maeve seemed to have a close affinity with one another and, when he was dying of cancer in 1959, she spent a great deal of time comforting him on his deathbed.

Arrival of a governess

Maeve was a precocious and feisty youngster which was hardly surprising in the circumstances having been left alone with her grandmother and far away from her parents. Children of Big Houses did not, as a rule and like other children, attend the local school. Gentry did not mix with the offspring of their tenants. They had governesses and one of those engaged for Maeve was an Englishwoman, Janet Clayton.

As she was travelling on the train from Dublin to Sligo to take up her post for the first time, she encountered in her compartment a chatty young boy who turned out to be Staskou who was returning from boarding school for his holiday at Lissadell. Miss Clayton was not met at the station by anyone representing her new employers. So she hired a pony and trap - and a most loquacious driver - and was entranced by the delights of the beautiful countryside on her way to Ardeevin. Immediately on her arrival she was assailed by a very spirited seven year old, Miss Maeve Alyss Markievicz, who proceeded to embarrass her new governess by showing off in front of a company of house guests. 'It is possible that Maeve's education was a problem'.[2]

At the start there was a love-hate relationship between governess and pupil. It was obvious to everyone that Maeve had one clear intention and that was to discomfit Miss Clayton as frequently as possible. In this endeavour, she succeeded - at least in the early days. Janet Clayton, however, was no shrinking violet having had considerable experience of other unruly and uncooperative children in her past positions. Maeve Markievicz would not get the better of this talented young woman who set about ensuring that her charge would learn, and learn quickly.

Lady Gore-Booth liked and respected Janet Clayton and gave her every support in the task of seeing that her granddaughter concentrated and paid attention to her lessons. However, when Constance came to see her mother and daughter on one of her fleeting and irregular visits, she accosted the new governess - 'so you are the hated Sassenach!'[3] Maeve had doubtless been in touch with her mother with news of the arrival of her governess.

Constance was rude and offhand in her initial dealings with Miss Clayton, but the latter was not intimidated or shocked by her outpourings. Although Constance had been snobbish and cutting with her daughter's new teacher, the governess had already known all about her pupil's absent mother and her nationalist politics and so she knew what to expect. Politics were never talked about at Ardeevin and Janet knew why. But she was able to weather the storm when confronted by such a notorious celebrity.

In later days, and in due course, Constance was greatly to appreciate the work done for, and the companionship given to, Maeve by Janet Clayton. Neither was it long before Maeve grew to greatly admire her governess and mentor. 'Miss Clayton quickly became a favourite, and she and Maeve settled down to a "happy, lively (sometimes truculent) schoolroom routine"'.[4] Maeve still had her moments, nonetheless, when she did twist her governess around her finger - 'Miss Clayton recalls that Maeve as she grew older was a better actress than her mother'.[5]

A routine was established at Ardeevin. Maeve would be required to attend lessons in the morning and early afternoon and Miss Clayton would then introduce her to the niceties of etiquette which were expected of a young lady of the Big House. Soon there was a second pupil for the governess - Stella L'Estrange. Stella was two years younger than Maeve and was the eldest child of the L'Estranges who were also relatives of the Gore-Booths living at Auburn House, just three short fields away from Ardeevin. These two young women became great friends as the years progressed and they both learned diligently under Miss Clayton's tutelage.

Maeve attended church on Sundays, sitting amongst the other members of the Gore-Booth family in their accustomed seats in Lissadell church. She would regularly visit her relatives at Lissadell and get to know the ever growing family of her younger cousins. They seemed to accept their older cousin although they were somewhat in awe of her. In the relatively early years of photography, there would have been snapshots of all the cousins taken at Lissadell and at Ardeevin along with their grandmother, their parents and all the other visitors to their homes. Maeve appeared comfortable in the company of Lady Gore-Booth at their home at Ardeevin.

Maeve aged 15

4

World War One and Turmoil in Ireland

Constance's dilemma: my country or my daughter?

The topsy-turvy life-style for Maeve continued. Whilst she remained at Ardeevin, in the company of her grandmother, her governess and the children closest to her - Stella and the older children of her uncle Josslyn and aunt Molly - life was irrevocably changing for her own parents and for Ireland in general. Nothing much was changing at Ardeevin and Lissadell, but back in Dublin Maeve's unpredictable mother was making a name for herself in nationalist circles.

Constance's Fianna Scouts were taking up much of her time and energy and her membership of Sinn Fein and 'The Daughters of Erin', for example, left no time whatsoever for thoughts of either husband or children. Contact between Constance and her family became more and more tenuous.

The Great Lock Out of 1913, when over 20,000 men became unemployed when locked out by their employers, gave Constance yet another focus and she worked night and day in the soup kitchens at Liberty Hall to feed the starving masses of the Dublin slums. She was in her element, although there were many detractors who hissed at her for her part in the rescue effort. Some refused to believe that this daughter of Lissadell could be involved for the people's benefit and did all they could to cast aspersions at the motivation for her actions. But she certainly worked hard and for many weeks during the strike and Lock Out she even slept at Liberty Hall.

Early in 1914, when the Lock Out eventually fizzled out and the men had been forced to return to work on worse, rather than better, terms, Constance was presented with an illuminated scroll by the poor women of the city for the part she had played to feed them during the crisis - much

to the chagrin of Delia Larkin, the sister of the great union leader, Jim Larkin.

When World War One broke out in the autumn of 1914, Ireland divided once more. The Ulster Volunteers were offered by Sir Edward Carson and Sir James Craig to the British war effort and large numbers of them went on to pay the ultimate sacrifice at the Battle of the Somme in July 1916.

The Irish Volunteers, by now split between those who supported John Redmond and those who had adhered to the more militant group under Eoin MacNeill, were themselves in a dilemma. In the end, Redmond offered his National Volunteers to the British war effort in his momentous and, for most people, damning speech at Woodenbridge, county Wicklow in September 1914. After that, there was no future for the exhausted and exasperated Irish Party leader and the way was left open for the more secretive and militant Irish Volunteers to take Ireland by storm.

The Easter Rising

This tempest erupted during Easter week 1916. Fearing that they might not actually manage to grasp the benefit of England's difficulty, Patrick Pearse, James Connolly and the military council of the Irish Republican Brotherhood seized Ireland's opportunity and led their meagre forces of less than 1,000 men and women into the jaws of the sleeping British giant on Easter Monday, 24 April 1916.

Throughout this short campaign, Constance Markievicz participated as the only woman to be commissioned in the Rising as a fighting soldier. She joined her commanding officer, the former British soldier and silk weaver Michael Mallin, resplendent in her uniform as an officer of the New Ireland, in St Stephen's Green during the afternoon of that fateful Easter Monday. With the sixty or seventy other combatants on the Green that day, she set about clearing the park of strollers, who had been enjoying a day out with their families, setting up barricades and digging trenches. Constance took a leading part in the organisation of what was to prove an impossible location to defend.

Because of their leader MacNeill's countermanding orders, which effectively greatly reduced the numbers who joined the rebels that day, there were not nearly sufficient fighters to hold the park and capture the high buildings, such as the Shelbourne Hotel, which surrounded it. The rebels, much to Constance's disappointment and embarrassment, were soon compelled to retreat ignominiously - and under cover of darkness - to the College of Surgeons on the west side of the Green.

To all intents and purposes, Constance's rebellion was over at that stage and, apart from firing shots at snipers from the roof of the college, she had just to wait for the end which even she knew would come sooner rather than later. The surrender, ordered by their commander-in-chief Patrick Pearse, came on the Saturday when Constance famously refused a lift in the car of the officer who had taken their surrender and instead marched off to Dublin Castle, head high, to the humiliation of surrender and defeat.

It was not long before a British court martial condemned her to death, the only woman to have been sentenced thus for her participation in the Rising. But the British had the final say. As Constance contemplated, with much pride and satisfaction, her death as a heroine of the rebellion, the news was quickly broken to her that, because she was a woman, her sentence had been commuted to penal servitude for life. She was not best pleased for she had looked forward to offering the ultimate sacrifice for her New Ireland which one day, she hoped, would be free of the hated British yoke.

Morning after morning, from 3 May, Constance listened to the rifle cracks which announced the deaths of the leaders of the rebellion. Patrick Pearse was the first to die. The last shots rang out on 12 May when her friend, mentor and the man she probably most admired, James Connolly, was dispatched seated on a chair, since his wounds incurred during the Rising prevented him from standing.

She was then transferred from Kilmainham jail to Mountjoy where she was left in solitary confinement until she was moved, at length, to Aylesbury prison in England. She was to languish there as the only Irish prisoner in that jail until June 1917 and she was the last of all the insurrectionists to be released from jail. Constance returned to Dublin in triumph with the cheering crowds surrounding her all the way from Dun Laoghaire to Dublin's city centre.

Maeve prepares to leave Ardeevin

Maeve was 14 years old at this time, with her own thoughts and apprehensions. The Gore-Booth family back at Lissadell certainly had problems in coming to terms with the rebellious Constance but they did their best to keep their private thoughts to themselves, not wishing to make a public spectacle of their displeasure.

At Ardeevin the dowager Lady Gore-Booth, although outwardly disapproving of her daughter's activities, nevertheless had no desire to sever her links with her eldest daughter. She had famously said, of Constance's exploits, 'Oh dear, oh dear, this will be the death of me some day'.[1]

Constance's brother, Sir Josslyn, was in an even more invidious position. His fellow landlords and gentlemen neighbours had plenty to say against their recalcitrant former friend, the firstborn daughter of Lissadell. They felt that there could be nothing severe enough for Constance for she had let down their class - the elite gentry of Ireland. Yet Sir Josslyn chose to steer a middle course. He felt obliged to condemn his sister's outrageous behaviour but he never disowned her.

At the time, Maeve was embarrassed and outraged by what she saw as her mother's folly. She refused to speak about her and did all she could to blot out Constance from her thoughts. 'She was estranged in spirit through indoctrination and absence. The immediate family...was appalled, concerned, or totally disapproving'.[2]

The only family member to stick by Constance through thick and thin was Maeve's Aunt Eva and it was she who made Constance's life tolerable during her lengthy periods of imprisonment and isolation. Constance herself, on smuggling out a letter from Aylesbury jail, thought that her daughter had been 'amused, not shocked'[3] by her part in the Rising. This was, perhaps, wishful thinking on Constance's behalf.

And yet, from her prison letters, Constance did occasionally give some thought to her daughter by requesting, for example, that a photograph of Maeve be sent to her in prison. Maeve sent a Christmas card to her mother and received a number of small gifts such as Easter eggs in return. These were nothing but insignificant and fleeting gestures from a distant and detached mother whose affections and passions were directed, not at her only child, but at an abstract view of mother Ireland.

The war effort in Sligo

Significantly the Easter Rising had taken place during World War One. The Big Houses of Ireland had firmly supported the British cause. The Big Houses of Ireland had sent their sons to war and lost scores of heirs and younger sons for what they saw as the cause of liberty. The ladies of the Big Houses, keeping a stiff upper lip, had supported the war effort by raising funds.

The dowager Lady Gore-Booth along with her daughter-in-law, Mary, played their parts admirably. During October 1916, for example, the two Sligo newspapers of the time, the *Sligo Champion* and the *Sligo Independent*, generously filled their columns advertising the forthcoming 'Children's Effort' which was a concert to be organised by Lady Gore-Booth and which was to take place in Sligo Town Hall on 20 and 21 October 1916. No one in the area could have failed to notice that this event was happening and for what purpose.

In the week after the concert, many more column inches were allocated to the minute description of the excellent performances by everyone involved. Maeve Markievicz, still at home under the wing of Miss Clayton, featured prominently in both parts of the concert. The papers offered fulsome congratulations for her recitation of 'The Pied Piper'. 'Her elocutionary powers call for special praise, and she was the recipient of the hearty plaudits of an enthusiastic audience. Her recitation, though somewhat long, never failed to please'.[4] According to the newspaper reports 'Miss de Markievicz was attired in a costume of a "mysterious old piper" and her make-up was splendid'.[5]

The second half of the concert was entirely devoted to a one act play, 'The Little Female Academy', which had been directed by Miss Clayton, whose untiring efforts in preparing the girls were duly reported - 'she worked ungrudgingly and that her efforts were rewarded there is not in the slightest doubt'.[6] In the play, Maeve and her friend, Stella L'Estrange, presented 'a charming song and dance'.[7]

This concert raised the excellent sum of £41/15/11 (£41.80) for the war workers' effort and, with reserved tickets costing 2/2 (11p) and unreserved ones at 1/1 (6p) both including war tax, was a successful conclusion to an enjoyable entertainment. Lady Gore-Booth was congratulated on her effort by the country newspapers in that obsequious way that local editors of the day were accustomed to doing.

Maeve and her friends and cousins were also aware of the calibre of Lady Gore-Booth's efforts in assisting local women to make money by acquiring new skills in the School of Needlework which she had started a number of years before the outbreak of the war. She employed a very talented teacher, Miss Flanagan, (an aunt of the artist, T.P. Flanagan) and the School's colourful brochure described the excellent needlework and embroidery pieces, such as sets of collar and cuffs from 2/6 (13p) which were sold to some very well known customers, who included the Princess of Wales and many other titled ladies.

During the Easter holidays in 1917 Maeve was again featuring in another fund-raising performance, this time at the home of Lieutenant Colonel and Mrs Campbell who owned a fine house called 'The Hermitage' not far from Lissadell near Calry church. It is in the newspaper report of this event that there is the first mention of Maeve playing the violin. During the performance she treated the audience to a violin solo which 'was received with great applause'.[8]

As time went on, Maeve became highly proficient on this instrument and eventually considered a career as a violinist although, as fate would have it, she was unable to pursue what could have been a very profitable profession.

School in England

At Ardeevin in the middle of 1917, with Janet Clayton continuing in her role as teacher, governess and confidante, the family decided that Maeve should be sent to school in England. Doubtless Constance and Casi might have had some say in the matter of their daughter's schooling during some of their earlier infrequent visits to Sligo and may have made their views known to Lady Gore-Booth.

In the ever changing circumstances, however, the decision was made by Gaga herself because neither Constance nor Casi was in a position to be thinking of their daughter's education in the midst of their own preoccupations. To the untrained and innocent eye it would seem that such a proposal to disrupt Maeve's life at the age of 15 and send her to England was heartless and unfeeling. She could now have every right to consider that her grandmother was also abandoning her as her mother and father had done in the past.

But she was now a mature young woman and she accepted the proposal with resignation. For the children of the gentry, attendance at a private or public school in England was simply the norm. Their pattern for education was clear; first of all a governess would teach the children the rudiments of education and then a private school would be chosen to which the children would be dispatched.

Maeve as a teenager

In the particular and unusual circumstances affecting Maeve - where Constance and Casi had long ago lost interest in their daughter - it seemed that a different course might conceivably have been thought more kind for her. She could not have been sent to school locally anyway as children from the Big House simply did not go to local schools. Although there were dissenting voices at Lady Gore-Booth's decision to send Maeve to England, they were efficiently and quickly silenced. Even some members of the family felt that the decision was a mistake.

Nonetheless, in the autumn term of 1917 when she was by now 15 and a half years old, Maeve was packed off to a very small private school in Hampshire. This was Barton Court School at New Milton, Hampshire, not far from the seaside resort of Bournemouth and its total complement throughout Maeve's sojourn there was never more than 24 pupils; 19 boarders and five day girls.

The school was a detached house with just three teachers and a headmistress. Maeve would have got very close and friendly with the other girls at the school although life must have been extremely claustrophobic for teenage girls in such confined and intense surroundings. It did become known amongst her school friends that Maeve's notorious mother had been involved in what they would have considered as the treachery of the 1916 Easter Rising in Dublin and occasionally she would have been referred to as 'That Woman's Daughter'. But Maeve was able to stand up for herself as she may have secretly admired her mother's independent streak.

She could also, of course, look forward to her holidays which she spent either back at Ardeevin with her grandmother and close to her cousins at Lissadell or with other relatives at such glamorous establishments as Naworth Castle, the home of the Earl of Carlisle, and Muncaster Castle, the elegant pile of the Earl of Scarborough. She enjoyed these vacations and her life was greatly enhanced by visits to these aristocratic houses where there were plenty of young people of her own age to join in various sports and social activities.

Maeve left Barton Court school at the end of the Easter term in 1919 and moved to Ivy House at Wimbledon Common in London. By now she was seventeen and a half years old and, although she only remained a pupil there for a little over a year, it was at this school that she perfected her skills in violin playing. She had already studied the instrument for a considerable time and was acknowledged to be a fine student. She gave various performances but, realising that a solo career was not a viable option and not wanting to end up playing second fiddle in an obscure string quartet somewhere, she gave up her musical ambitions early on.

At this time her grandmother, still very much one of the landed gentry, was looking forward to having her granddaughters presented at Court. However, although Maeve was by now a very fine looking young woman and eminently suitable for presentation to the sovereign, Lady Gore-Booth reluctantly decided that, in view of Constance's rebellious activities, it would not be prudent to proceed with the ceremony. Maeve was not at all concerned and was pleased with Gaga's decision. There would now be no requirement to practise her curtsies!

Maeve's schooling was complete by the summer of 1920 and she now had to give some thought to earning a living.

5

The Family is Dispersed

While Maeve was at home at Ardeevin and participating in her grandmother's concerts in Sligo during the autumn of 1916, Constance was being held prisoner in Aylesbury prison. Her name was barely mentioned at home although Constance, in her letters from prison, showed that she had not entirely forgotten her teenage daughter. Her correspondence was almost exclusively sent to her sister, Eva, who retained a very close link with the 'black sheep' of the family.

But, when Constance was sent to Holloway jail in May 1918, she never once mentioned Maeve in any of her letters right up to the date of her release from there in March 1919. However, while Constance was 'on the run' from the British authorities and successfully running her Ministry of Labour, under most trying circumstances in 1920, she saw Maeve on a number of occasions, telling Eva, 'Maeve herself is very busy. She seems quite fit and well and is looking lovely, though thin'.[1] Constance was eventually tracked down by the authorities and sent to prison yet again, this time to Mountjoy for ten months.

During 1920, when Maeve was a pupil at Ivy House and was playing violin solos, Constance enquired of Eva what she thought of her daughter's ability on the instrument. 'You did not tell me what you thought of Maeve's music. Is there a spark in it? I never care for mere technique. I suppose she is in a state of being wildly amused and interested in life'.[2] But, as we now know, nothing became of this possible career path.

The entire relationship between Constance and Maeve had never been that of mother and daughter. Constance treated Maeve as an adult - a fact which had exacerbated the emotional chasm between them when Maeve was a child. She had been starved of motherly affection in her formative years which made any real and lasting relationship difficult, if not impossible.

Constance, Maeve and Eva

A portrait of Staskou taken in 1915

Staskou Markievicz

Maeve's stepbrother, Staskou, had left his boarding school, Mount St Benedict's in Gorey, county Wexford, in 1913 and had enrolled at the Berlitz School in Dublin's Grafton Street to study French and Russian. Two years later, in 1915, he left Dublin to fulfil the long-standing promise that had been made by Constance and Casi to his paternal grandmother in Poland that he would return there after he had finished his schooling.

His return journey through Russia was chaotic. By now he could scarcely speak any Russian or Polish and yet he had to make his way through submarine infested seas and across the arctic wastes of northern Europe in military and Red Cross trains to reach Russia and thence to Poland.

Upon arrival he joined the Polish army and was injured in the fighting during the Russian campaign. He was looked upon as nothing more than 'meat for the guns' as recruits were then called. But after the war his fortunes had changed. There had been some correspondence between Maeve and himself when Maeve was at school in England and it was evident that Staskou was having difficulties in readjusting to life as a civilian. Many of his problems over the years revolved around money - or the lack of it.

Although accurate information is vague, it seems that Staskou may have married young - rather like his father and mother - around 1922 in Poland. He may even have had a baby daughter who had died as an infant. Constance, in a letter to him written aboard a train whilst she was travelling on a lecture tour of America in May 1922, asked him for 'more information' about his wife'.[3] He had also been imprisoned by the Bolsheviks from 1921-1922 and had endured suffering whilst in captivity and Constance was concerned how he had managed to overcome his privations.

She was anxious to persuade him to emigrate to America where she was convinced that he would do well. By using her not inconsiderable influence, she told Staskou that she could easily get a job for him. Subsequently, in later correspondence, during the cruel early days of the Irish Free State, she told him that his mastery of languages could land him a responsible post within the new administration in Dublin. Staskou cherished these letters which reminded him of happier days in Dublin when he was a carefree youngster.

Casimir, 1913

Casimir's war service

Staskou's father, Casimir, had been in Italy when the Great War broke out and later had been a war correspondent for a number of English newspapers in the Balkans. He had subsequently enlisted 'with his usual enthusiasm for any adventure'[4] and had joined his regiment, the 12th Regiment of the Hussars, in their campaign against the Austrians in the Carpathian mountains through the bitter 1915/1916 winter.

After some months he was wounded by shrapnel and, just as he was recovering, he then contracted typhus. He hovered between life and death but eventually recovered, much to the doctors' relief and surprise. He had also been decorated for his bravery. Having fully convalesced at his family home, he had sent a letter to Constance during 1916 telling her about his wartime experiences and also informing her that he had rekindled his interest in plays and was putting on productions in Moscow and in Kiev. He had also taken up painting once more. Yet he was not to write to his wife again until the middle of 1921 following the Truce which eventually brought an end to the War of Independence in Ireland.

For Maeve the immediate family was little more than a broken reed. There were no letters from her parents or from Staskou. She would now have to make her own way in the world without any help, interest or guidance from her family.

Taking time to decide

For three years, whilst her mother was enduring many terms of imprisonment in England, Dublin and Cork, Maeve rarely saw Constance. She had returned from school and lived, for a short period of time, at Ardeevin with Lady Gore-Booth.

In 1922 Constance was in America on a speaking tour to promote her republican ideals, having been sent there by Eamon de Valera in the company of Kathleen Barry (the sister of the young medical student, Kevin Barry, condemned to death and executed by the British on 1 November 1920). Constance was, as ever, excited in her new found role as travelling ambassador for the anti-Treaty faction in Ireland as she enthralled and transfixed her American audiences with her radical style of oratory.

She liked to style herself 'Constance, Countess de Markievicz' which greatly attracted the Americans who never failed to be drawn to an

Irish speaker, especially one who was a woman, and a noblewoman into the bargain.

During the long and arduous train journeys criss-crossing that vast country, Kathleen Barry never ceased to be amazed at Constance's almost naïve description of 'my little daughter'. When she was buying presents for Maeve - including, it seems, Hudson Bay furs - Kathleen expected Maeve to be much younger than she was, simply because of the way Constance spoke about her. When Maeve turned up in London for a reunion with her mother on their return from America, Kathleen met a tall young woman of 20 years, and not the youngster she had imagined by Constance's description of her. It had been three years since mother and daughter had last met at Cork jail and, after Maeve had been introduced to Kathleen, she had to ask her to point out her mother in a group of women talking in the hotel foyer.

However, despite the vagaries of their unpredictable relationship over the years, Maeve and her mother did become reconciled to a certain degree. Maeve had spent some of her time in Ireland after the conclusion of her horticulture course in 1922 until her grandmother's death early in 1927 and she saw Constance in Dublin on several occasions. 'She was at least making up for lost time with Maeve whom she now saw fairly regularly'.[5]

Constance was delighted that she was seeing more of Maeve and took pride in what her daughter could achieve and how well she was looking. 'Maeve spent a day here on her way to Sligo and helped me pull the car to pieces. She loves machinery and is very clever at it. She is very tall and pretty and full of life and charm'.[6] On another occasion she was obviously equally delighted to see her daughter when she quipped to Eva in one of the last letters sent to her, 'Maev (sic) blew in on her way to Sligo and commandeered the car'.[7]

They were evidently enjoying each other's company and Maeve revelled in the opportunity to meet her mother and borrow her old 'Tin Lizzie' Ford car. Maeve clearly enjoyed driving in those relatively early days of the motor car. Although there was not a car at Ardeevin, her uncle Josslyn had been one of the first people in Sligo to invest in the century's latest contraption. He had bought, as far back as 1906, a splendid French Torrean car and had also acquired at the same time, by dint of his persistence, a chauffeur to drive it. Albert Barnard had been sent across to Ireland to deliver the car and had given in to Sir Josslyn's pleadings for a person to drive and look after the new automobile. He was to stay at

Lissadell for many years. The car was changed for a 1908 Wolseley model which became a long-time favourite of the family. These new motorcars regularly transported the Gore-Booths on their trips to their holiday home, 'Seaview West', in Bundoran in county Donegal and on fishing trips to the river Erne and further afield.

When Maeve left Ivy House school her grandmother, after firmly deciding against having her very handsome granddaughter presented as a debutante at Court along with her English cousins, had her enrolled at the Swanley Horticultural College in Kent with a view to Maeve pursuing a profession in landscape gardening. She had demonstrated her expertise at home and had learnt much from her talented uncle Josslyn who was an expert in seeds and bulbs in his workshops and greenhouses at Lissadell. Sir Josslyn had immersed himself in the intricacies of propagating new strains of various bulbs and his name had become renowned and respected amongst those interested in this branch of horticulture.

On completion of her course at Swanley, having graduated with a BSc (Hort.) degree, Maeve felt confident that she had chosen her calling wisely and spent the four succeeding years undertaking posts in practical farming. She then took up an appointment as a member of staff at the Darlington Training School for Teachers imparting her gardening skills to the students there. By the end of the 1920s, however, she had left this position, although for the next two decades and more she pursued her chosen career. But within a few years of completely settling down, her life was yet further disrupted.

Family bereavements

In June 1926, Maeve's Aunt Eva died in England. She had been a woman devoted to the needs of the poor and downtrodden for many years. She had alleviated the lives of factory workers in the slums of Manchester and the surrounding towns by assiduously working to have legislation introduced to improve their working conditions. Along with her lifelong friend and companion, Esther Roper, Eva Gore-Booth had become one of the first social workers whom Great Britain had known.

In her early days she had even enlisted the help of Constance in the pursuit of better terms and working conditions for the pub girls of Manchester. And in pursuit of that cause, she had contributed to the defeat of Winston Churchill in a parliamentary election in 1908.

Eva was also a celebrated poet and had published many books of poetry and verse. She was certainly not a typical Gore-Booth and, like her sister Constance, Eva had turned her back on the life of style and elegance which was typically the lot of most daughters of the Irish gentry.

However, Eva Gore-Booth will always be remembered as the one member of the Gore-Booth family who remained constant and faithful to the unconventional Constance Markievicz. These two sisters had an undying love for one another and there was an affinity which could even be described as a mystical bond between them. Although Eva and Constance were not often actually in each other's company, they were regularly in touch with one another.

When Constance was incarcerated in various jails between 1916 and 1923, the one person she wrote to was Eva. There were countless letters written between the two women and when Constance needed something done, she turned to Eva in the certain knowledge that it would be done. Whenever Maeve's name was mentioned in these letters it was always Eva who saw to it that Constance's requests in regard to her daughter were fulfilled. Eva was a true and trustworthy sister and, without her, Constance would have been almost totally friendless.

In fact when Eva died in 1926, Constance could not bring herself to attend the funeral fearing a backlash from members of the family. She was devastated and heartbroken and her sister's death left her seriously contemplating her own mortality. The touching story is told that she was discovered in a darkened room in the house she lived in with the Coghlan family in floods of tears shortly after Eva's passing. In truth, the tough and feisty Constance of bygone years had become frail and vulnerable knowing that she would no longer have her remarkable sister's counsel to rely upon.

Maeve had not known her aunt very well yet mourned her loss. She realised how much the loss would affect her mother - and then there was the reality that her elderly grandmother had lost the first of her offspring.

Sadly Georgina, Lady Gore-Booth herself died on 23 January 1927, aged 85, at Ardeevin. She was laid to rest in the secluded and private Gore-Booth family plot in the church grounds beside her husband, Sir Henry, who had died 27 years previously. It was a wet and wintry day as the final obsequies were performed by the Reverend Samuel Miller after the service in Lissadell church. The mourning family members attended and there, in their midst, was Constance Markievicz and her daughter,

Maeve. Constance looked wretched and lonely. Within the space of only a few months, the two members of her family who had stuck closest to her over the recent years of turmoil, were dead. 'Madame was in Sligo that dark January when her mother was buried in the Lissadell churchyard'.[8]

Maeve herself had lost the family member who was closest to her - her beloved grandmother who had, so many years ago, taken the place of her mother. She felt bereft and lonely and, in the dozens of letters of sympathy sent to Sir Josslyn and his wife, Maeve's name is mentioned by so many of the family friends as being the person who would most miss Lady Gore-Booth. This was indeed the stark reality for Maeve for she now felt totally on her own.

As far back as 1906, Lady Gore-Booth had made her will. Around that time she had moved to Ardeevin leaving her son Sir Josslyn, then as yet unmarried, at Lissadell. She decided to leave all her money and property to Maeve, who was still a minor at the time. She was to be the sole beneficiary.

Although Lady Gore-Booth was to have twelve more grandchildren, she had chosen to leave everything to Maeve, the child upon whom she had doted particularly in her early years when Constance and Casi had effectively abandoned her. She never changed her will as her remaining grandchildren were born between 1906 and 1920, when Angus, her last grandchild, was born. It probably never occurred to Josslyn, Mabel and Mordaunt that their mother had any intention of leaving all her possessions, including the house at Ardeevin, to the one and only offspring of their headstrong sister. It may have been, however, that Constance herself had some inkling of her mother's intentions but she never shared the information with anyone. In addition to leaving Ardeevin to Maeve, her grandmother had also left her a rather insignificant amount of money - just £1,786.

The death of Constance

It was also unfortunate timing that the last will and testament of Georgina, dowager Lady Gore-Booth, was arranged to be read some months after her death in the early summer of that fateful year. For in July 1927, the third death in the Gore-Booth family in the space of a little over twelve months occurred.

Constance, by now 59 years old and tired and worn out by her frantic endeavours to bring fuel to the poor and needy in the slums of Dublin, fell ill. Feeling unwell whilst attending a Fianna Fail executive meeting in Dublin, she was admitted to Sir Patrick Dun's hospital and was diagnosed with appendicitis. She had specifically requested that, as she could afford no other hospital, - 'I am a pauper'[9] - she be admitted to this Dublin hospital traditionally used by the city's poor and destitute. Constance even went into a public ward, although there were many who would have seen to it that she had a private room.

The first operation, performed by the eminent Dublin surgeon, Sir William Taylor, appeared to be successful and she was in good spirits. But peritonitis set in and a second operation had to be performed. This time the outcome seemed less certain. Constance was struggling for her life and, on 7 July, radio broadcast messages were transmitted by the BBC to summon her daughter, husband and stepson to her bedside.

The situation was critical and her Dublin friends kept vigil awaiting the arrival of her nearest family members. Helena Moloney, Marie Perolz and Hanna Sheehy Skeffington, stalwarts of the many women's organisations, like the Daughters of Erin to which they all belonged, comforted their friend. Dr Kathleen Lynn, who had fought with her during the Easter Rising, held her hand and whispered reassuring words to her and May Coghlan, with whom Constance had lived for some time past, remained constantly by her side. But the unspoken fear amongst all her dear friends in those last hours was whether or not Maeve, Casi and Staskou would arrive in time.

But the emergency broadcast messages had done their work. Maeve was first to arrive, having come from her training college in Darlington. Newspaper reports announced that she had arrived in Dublin and that the news of her mother's sudden illness, which had been broadcast from the London station on the previous Thursday night, had come as a great shock to her.

Soon Esther Roper, Eva's constant companion throughout her life, arrived from London. And, as if by a miracle on the morning of Monday 11 July, Casi and Staskou appeared having somehow heard the message in Poland. Staskou 'was aghast at the change that her illness and terrible experiences had wrought; one could hardly recognise that this was the same person - except for those keen blue eyes, which lighted up at the sight of us'.[10] It had been twelve years since he had seen Constance.

It was a poignant moment as the once fiery and indomitable Constance lay on her death bed - little more than the fragile shadow of her former self. Surrounded by flowers, mainly her favourite roses, she could only look upon her family gathered around her - those dearest to her whom she had shunned and deserted to follow her republican ideals. She exclaimed that 'this is the happiest day of my life! You are just the same - haven't changed at all'.[11]

During the late hours of 14 July, Constance's condition became serious and Sir William informed the family that her life was in danger. With the family around her, Constance Markievicz died at 1.30 on the morning of Friday 15 July 1927. The Gore-Booths at Lissadell had to be informed by a member of the L'Estrange family who lived at Lisnalurg House close to Ardeevin. Their telephone was in their house whereas the one at Lissadell was in the offices in the outbuildings. Consequently they had to rely on their L'Estrange relations coming round the eight miles on a pony and trap to inform them of Constance's passing.

The three great Gore-Booth women of that generation, Constance, Eva and their mother Georgina, Lady Gore-Booth, were dead - and all within the space of just one year.

Constance Markievicz's funeral took place on Sunday 17 July to Glasnevin cemetery after a lying in state at the Rotunda. Not even for such a person as Constance Markievicz would the City fathers allow the use of the Mansion House for this purpose. Neither did the fledgling Free State government want to risk outrage and chaos following the very recent assassination and burial of their own Cabinet colleague, Kevin O'Higgins, just a few days previously.

However, thousands of ordinary Dubliners and many of the slum dwellers she had helped so much lined the route, tears welling up in their eyes, their heads bared to the elements. Her family and friends followed the cortege in coaches, draped in black trimmings. Several coach loads full of flowers followed in their train but, on the coffin itself, there lay just one floral tribute - from Constance's husband, daughter and stepson.

Casi, Staskou and Maeve had been joined by Sir Josslyn and Lady Gore-Booth. Many had remarked at the appearance of the head of the family, but it is to Sir Josslyn's eternal credit that he made sure to attend the final chapter of the life of a sister who had caused the family so much pain and heartache. He and his wife saw it as their duty to support Constance's family in their time of grief. Although Casi, Maeve and Staskou would have wanted a private funeral, they realised that this could never have been possible owing to Constance's high republican profile. Consequently they would have found the whole day very depressing.

It was Eamon de Valera who delivered the graveside oration. He intoned 'Madame Markievicz is gone from us; Madame, the friend of the toiler, the lover of the poor. Ease and station she put aside, and took the hard way of service with the weak and the downtrodden. Sacrifice, misunderstanding and scorn lay on the road she adopted, but she trod it unflinchingly'.[12]

This was, of course, the same de Valera who had fought in the Rising but who had not been sentenced to death for his part in it as Constance had been. His American connections had saved him from the firing squad. This was the same de Valera who had appointed Constance Markievicz as the first woman ever to have a place in a government Cabinet, albeit one not recognised by the British. This was the same de Valera who had sent Constance off to America on a lecture tour to promote his own political ideals.

Constance was not buried until the next day as gravediggers did not work on Sundays. Even then, surrounded as she was by her Fianna Scouts, the nervous government insisted on no volley being fired over the grave. The Last Post was sounded and the rebellious daughter of Lissadell was laid to rest.

Throughout all these ceremonies, Maeve contemplated what might have been. Her recent contacts with her mother had been more felicitous for it had suited Constance to be dealing with an adult and not with a child. She had always seemed strangely devoid of maternal love and emotion for Maeve in her early days. Maeve looked on to see how devoted the very ordinary people were to her mother - one born into privilege, yet dying into poverty. She had lost her grandmother and now her mother. Ireland would never again hold any attraction to her, except fleetingly, in the latter days of her own life.

6

Maeve Leaves Ireland

After the funeral in Dublin, Casi and Staskou remained in Ireland for a short visit. They saw the Gore-Booths again and spent some time with Maeve. Yet when they were ready to return to Poland, they realised how much of a stranger Maeve had become to them. Her attitude to her Polish relations was remote and cold. From then on it was clear that contact between her father and stepbrother would remain strained. This was to prove correct. Maeve had more of her mother's independence and none of her father's innate coyness and timidity. Even relations with Staskou took a decided downturn.

Staskou had returned to Poland before his father or Maeve left Ireland after Constance's funeral. Maeve had clearly decided that, with her grandmother and mother now both dead, she would finally kick the dust of Ireland from off her feet. Her attitude was only too obvious as to her thoughts about the country of her birth. The story is told that, as she and Casi left Dun Laoghaire by ferry, she had turned to her father and forcefully stated that she would never want to set foot in Ireland again. An indignant fellow passenger had overheard and taken umbrage telling her, in no uncertain terms, that she should never have come to Ireland in the first place. The incident showed Maeve's insensitive streak and her father's reticence and embarrassment. Maeve was rarely seen in Ireland again for many years.

A home in Kent

By the middle of 1928, Maeve had sold Ardeevin and had funds to purchase her own home in England. She decided to live in Kent. A house called Verrall's Oak in the village of Egerton, near Ashford, came on the market and Maeve bought it. This two storey house was a large detached red-bricked dwelling with an ample garden and splendid orchards. It was in the middle of the lush Kent countryside and was ideal for Maeve to pursue her career in landscape gardening. She had lots of mature apple trees and space to cultivate vegetables and flowers.

Her first problem, however, was to arrange for her furniture to be shipped from Sligo. In a series of letters to Mrs Hanna Sheehy Skeffington, who was an executrix of her mother's will, Maeve explained the arrangements which she had made with a firm of furniture removers called Beverly and Smyth who had agreed to ship her belongings at the end of July. In those days the rate for a one way removal from Ireland to the south of England was the sum total of £33.

Maeve asked Mrs Sheehy Skeffington to supervise the removal, for she did not want to come over herself unless absolutely necessary because of what she considered to be the expensive cost of travelling to Ireland. Most of the furniture was, by that time, in Dublin although there were still items which needed moved from Ardeevin, including her bed. Maeve had given instructions that the removers had to take great care in packing some large canvasses which had been painted by Casi and Constance. She had told Mrs Sheehy Skeffington that 'I shall be taking father's pictures as I am sure he will never send for them and as my house has big rooms they will look very nice on the walls'.[1]

Maeve was contemplating taking her father's paintings without having sought his permission. They included Casi's 'Bread' triptych which was of some considerable value. Included in her father's pictures was, in all likelihood, Constance's well known painting 'The Conscript'.

Shortly after the date of Maeve's letter of 6 July 1928, Mrs Sheehy Skeffington would appear to have been in touch with Casimir in Poland and, in anticipation of his reply, she had written to Maeve asking her to postpone the removal arrangements, without presumably telling her the reason for the postponement. However a telegram from Darlington, dated 20 July, 1928, arrived with Mrs Sheehy Skeffington - 'Sorry cannot postpone; writing, Markievicz'.[2] Maeve followed this up with a letter explaining that it would be impossible to postpone the arrangements as it was now going to take up to ten days to effect the removal and that she did not want the expense of having to put up in a hotel for the duration.

Maeve then received a telegram from Mrs Sheehy Skeffington which said - 'Count writes forbidding removal large pictures. Instructing Beverly Smyth accordingly writing, Skeffington'.[3]

The mystery of where the pictures actually went, however, does appear to have been resolved some years later in a letter dated 26 September 1933 which Staskou had written to an old friend in Dublin, Tommy Smyth.

Verrall's Oak, Egerton

'The George' and St James' Parish Church, Egerton

Maeve de Markievicz and Master Aubrey Wells, May Festival, Egerton (c.1934)

Mary James, wearing Constance Markievicz's wedding veil

In it, Staskou, who was in financial difficulties at the time, told Tommy that Maeve had got rid of everything of her mother's that she did not want, as she was the sole beneficiary of her will. She had disposed of the piano and her old Ford car although, Staskou went on to say, his father had laid claims to a number of items including the paintings which he had executed and also some of Constance's.

Casi was dead by this time and Staskou wanted some of these artefacts to clear his father's debts. Maeve had held on to the paintings and Mrs Sheehy Skeffington's efforts at postponing the removal (which included the pictures) had failed.

Maeve's attitude to her late mother's dear friend, Mrs May Coghlan, (with whom Constance had lived for the last years of her life) showed a callous disregard for the service rendered by the Coghlans to Constance. In her first letter to Mrs Sheehy Skeffington, Maeve said how kind the family had been in housing much of her furniture, and yet complained that they owed her £30. Maeve said she would cancel this debt if the Coghlans gave her back the piano which she had originally told them they could keep. Maeve was annoyed that Mrs Coghlan had not replied to her letter and considered them ungrateful since they had had the use of the furniture until such time as it had to be removed to England. Mrs Sheehy Skeffington's views on how the matter should be resolved were sought earnestly by Maeve. No answer was ever given.

Hanna Sheehy Skeffington had always been a great friend of Constance's. They had campaigned over many issues and had spent time in jail together. Mrs Sheehy Skeffington had called Constance, on many occasions, 'Ireland's "Joan of Arc"'. When she died, it seemed natural that such an able and loyal friend should become executrix to her will. Owing to Constance's most complicated comings and goings, particularly over her last years, the administration of the will took more than a year to resolve.

But to Hanna it was a labour of love and, throughout the rest of her life, she kept the memory of Constance Markievicz fresh by continuing to write regular articles in the journals and newspapers about her dear friend. Consequently the somewhat officious attitude of Maeve in their recent dealings caught in her throat. There was no love lost between this renowned Irish feminist and the high-handed daughter of her dearest companion. Some years later she heard that Maeve was contemplating writing a biography of her mother. Mrs Sheehy Skeffington was most indignant declaring that Maeve was the last person to be writing about Constance.

Settling down at Verrall's Oak

Maeve had chosen well in her decision to live in Egerton. It is the archetypal village lying in the idyllic apple county of Kent. Its beautiful village green is overlooked by the elegant tower of the 13th century parish church of St James the Great. The village pub, 'the George', stands close by beside the village shop. The pub has always been the focal point of life in Egerton and it certainly was in the days when Maeve was resident in the village.

Verrall's Oak, part Tudor and with a 1710 Queen Anne frontage, lies just down the hill from the church on Stonebridge Green Road and was the home of Maeve Markievicz from 1928 until 1939. She bought it for the princely sum of £500 and, in addition to the house itself, she came into possession of a grain store, a barn and some other small outhouses. With the property also came twenty acres of land with orchards and ample space for vegetable growing and paddocks where animals could graze.

Not long after taking over Verrall's Oak, Maeve employed a local man, Albert Smith, to assist her in the garden. Much hard work was needed to bring this large garden into shape to enable her to grow produce for the open market. There already were apples in abundance and soon flower beds and vegetable patches were prepared. A large field at the rear of the property was turned over to the cultivation of blackcurrants and the harvesting of these in July each year was always a considerable effort, although Maeve was always helped in this mammoth task by many of the villagers. She is still remembered by many in Egerton as being a gifted and enthusiastic gardener.

Maeve sold the flowers from her extensive garden to many local outlets. She was talented in botany and horticulture, skills which she had obtained at the Swanley College and from her uncle Josslyn at Lissadell. She kept pigs, too, and also produced a great deal of home made jam. By the mid 1930s she had embarked upon another venture - that of confectionary making.

Village life

In the early 1930s, Maeve became the chairman of the Egerton Village Gardeners' Society. She exhibited much of her produce and flowers at the annual village horticultural show and often was asked to judge some of the classes. Upon relinquishing the chairmanship of the Society in 1932, she presented a suitably inscribed silver rose bowl which is still, to this day, in the possession of an Egerton villager, Miss Doreen E. Weeks, a prize which had been won by her father at the show that year.

Maeve quickly became involved in village life. Each year she invited the senior pupils at the local school to come to her orchard and harvest the crop. She then generously donated the apples to the remainder of the school children to take home to their parents. It is clear from this regular act of kindness that she did not make much money from her abundant apple crops. Although there was a ready market for Kent apples, she profited little from their sale.

The older boys at the school also each had a vegetable plot there and every year they were delighted to hear that Miss de Markievicz was again coming to judge the best plot. She was always considered to be a fair competition adjudicator and her talents were appreciated by both pupils and teachers alike. Everyone was happy with the outcome of the competition.

Within a short time, Maeve became a well-known figure in Egerton. She was seen as an eccentric. She was a tall, striking-looking woman often dressed in trousers - which, in the 1930s, turned many heads and was, to say the least, an unusual form of dress for the fairer sex. She also smoked and drank and even wore make-up.

She owned a rather splendid light blue foreign motor car with a black canvas hood which was regularly parked in crazy angles in various parts of the village, more often than not outside 'the George'. The car was known to have careered down one of the village hills when Maeve had not properly applied the handbrake. It seems that she even had a motor cycle for some of the time. 'Many people were in awe of her commanding presence, and she was regarded as a 'character', whose offers of lifts were usually refused because the experience of being driven by her was too hair-raising!'[4]

Maeve organised a small village band which performed at various local events in the village. Practices were held in the upstairs room of the former grain store at Verrall's Oak and it was not unheard of for Maeve to loudly castigate members who arrived late for practice. Many of the performers, including Dudley (later Sir Dudley) Harmer, were acknowledged as extremely talented musicians in their own right.

The band played at various local events in the village hall and in the church, and many recall it playing at the Silver Jubilee celebrations for King George V and Queen Mary in 1935. She was a member of the village committee which organised the celebrations for King George VI and Queen Elizabeth on their Coronation Day, 12 May 1937. Egerton's festivities commenced that day at 8 a.m. with Communion in the Parish Church and ended with the lighting of a bonfire at 9.30 p.m. and, during the afternoon and evening, it was noted in the Egerton Coronation Celebrations Souvenir Programme of 12 May 1937 that Miss de Markievicz's Coronation band played suitable selections throughout the day.

On many occasions, therefore, 'she thrilled the villagers with her violin playing and it was generally known that she wanted to become a professional violinist but gave up the idea as her talents did not lie in that direction'.[5]

During the 1930s, Maeve tried her hand at many other different types of hobbies and leisure pursuits. She enjoyed music and wrote some poetry as well as getting marginally involved in film making and writing a detective novel. Although she made little or no progress in these activities, nonetheless it showed that her mind was continually active and that she was keen to dabble in a great variety of interesting pastimes.

She was a friendly person who moved freely amongst the people of the village with her seven, rather snappy, Scottie dogs. Maeve was also a member of the village dramatic society and once she had to be persuaded not to appear in a particular play with her dogs. The thought of several unruly dogs careering across the stage was too much for the other members to contemplate - although the idea had certainly appealed to the flamboyant Miss de Markievicz!

But life at Verrall's Oak was not all work and community involvement. Maeve often invited friends to come and stay and a number of Irish friends and cousins regularly appeared. On long, hot summer days, Maeve and her companion at that time, Edith Keable - a small, placid and good-natured woman known as 'auntie' (although she was perhaps only a few years older than Maeve) - lay around in their garden with their friends and their Scottie dogs.

Stella L'Estrange, who was then living in London, was a regular visitor as were her Lissadell cousins, Rosaleen and Bridget Gore-Booth. A number of men friends from Ireland also called and stayed at Verrall's Oak in those halcyon days prior to the outbreak of war and, on at least one occasion, some of her Polish relatives visited.

Maeve was 35 years old by the mid 1930s. Life in Kent seemed to agree with her. Maeve made many visits in her car to the seaside with her visitors to the little seashore changing huts at Camber on the English Channel coast.

EGERTON
CORONATION
CELEBRATIONS

May 12th, 1937.

SOUVENIR PROGRAMME

Newton Clark, Charing and Willesborough.

PROGRAMME

8.0 a.m.   Communion Service in Parish Church
9.0 a.m.   Peal of Bells
10.30 a.m.   Wireless Broadcast in Parish Church
2.30 p.m. Service in the Church
                        (Collection in Church for British Legion)
3.20 p.m. Tree Planting Ceremony in Churchyard
3.30 p.m. Meet at the Village Hall
                        Hoist Union Jack
                        Sing "God Save the King"
3.45 p.m. Presentation to School Children
4.0 p.m.   Children's Tea in the Village Hall
4.30-6 p.m.   Treasure Hunt followed by Children's Sports
4.30-6 p.m.   Teas for Parishioners
6.0 p.m.   Fancy Dress Parade for Children
6.15 p.m. Sports for Adults
7.30 p.m. Fancy Head-dress Parade for Ladies
7.45 p.m. Dancing in the Village Hall
9.30 p.m. Light Bonfire

During the Afternoon and Evening Miss de Markievicz's CORONA-
TION BAND will play suitable selections.

British Legion Emblems will be sold by Members of the Egerton
Branch Women's Institute.

President :
Major C. H. STISTED.

Chairman :
W. ROY WILTHEW, Esq.

Vice-Chairman :
Rev. L. C. Luckraft

Committee :

Mr. J. H. Harrison. Mrs. Ray Gore.
Mr. L. H. Hopkins. Mrs. E. J. Berridge.
Mr. S. H. Field.   Miss M. de Markievicz.
Mr. P. Oliver.   Mrs. C. Raines,
Mr. Jeffrey Pack.   Mrs. H. Smith.
Miss E. Waterhouse

Hon. Secretary
Mr. E. J. Berridge

She employed Mary James (née Russell) as a maid to look after her house. Mary recalled that, as a teenager, she worked for Maeve from 1932 until 1934. She liked her employer very much although she admitted that Miss de Markievicz 'used to drink and hide the bottles from her companion'.[6] She always received her pay at the end of every week and, when it was raining, she was taken home by Maeve in her very grand motor car. A few years later, after she had stopped working for Maeve, Mary got married in the village church and Maeve insisted that she wore the one hundred year-old wedding veil which her own mother, Constance, had worn at her wedding back in 1900. Little did Mary realise the significance of wearing a veil used by one of Ireland's foremost heroines.

During the 1930s Maeve also kept in touch with Sir Josslyn and Lady Gore-Booth's sons, Hugh and Brian. They both lived and worked within easy striking distance of Kent and Maeve enjoyed their occasional visits to Verrall's Oak.

A precarious financial hold

Running a business selling fruit and flowers proved to be a shaky financial existence for Maeve Markievicz. At least the house at Verrall's Oak was her own through the beneficence of her late grandmother and the sale of Ardeevin. Particularly at this time, money matters were foremost in Maeve's mind.

In July 1928, as she was making arrangements for her furniture to be removed to Kent, Maeve had requested her solicitors, Baddeley and Co., to credit her account at Coutts Bank with the dividends on a number of securities which stood in the name of Hanna Sheehy Skeffington and her uncle, Mordaunt Gore-Booth. These stocks were considerable and included £1,750 in the Great Northern Railway; £400 in Dublin United Tramways; nearly £3,000 in Great Southern Railways and £64 in the Clogher Valley Railway. The executors readily agreed to Maeve's request and, from then on, the dividends accruing year on year went direct to Maeve, thus giving her another regular source of income.

Maeve was also in receipt of a monthly allowance from the Gore-Booths at Lissadell and she kept regular contact by letter with Sir Josslyn. She often seemed to be short of money and relied upon her Irish payment to supplement her income from the sale of goods and produce from the garden at Verrall's Oak. She tended to be rather unbusinesslike which resulted in her finances often being in a muddle.

Although her business at her garden centre did have some profitable times, it was clear that her schemes for making a living were sporadic, to say the least. Her business acumen appeared to lack sound judgment when an ability to diversify could well have improved her financial lot. Living in England might have had some advantages for Maeve, but she was still reliant on regular financial assistance from Ireland. She had not been able, try as she might, to totally forget her Irish roots.

7

A Family Biography of Constance

It took seven long years for the first biography of Constance Markievicz to be written and published. Sean O Faolain, well known in literary circles in Dublin, had written his book, 'Constance Markievicz or the Average Revolutionary', in 1934. The Gore-Booths, as well as Maeve and Staskou, disliked and despised the book in every shape and form. Staskou called it 'an awful parody'.

Other biographies were subsequently written and it was over thirty years before Anne Marreco wrote 'The Rebel Countess - the Life and Times of Constance Markievicz' and Jacqueline Van Voris 'Constance de Markievicz, in the Cause of Ireland' both in 1967. Then in 1987 and 1988 respectively, further biographies by Diana Norman, 'Terrible Beauty, a Life of Constance Markievicz', and Anne Haverty, 'Constance Markievicz, an Independent Life', appeared.

But in the early days after Constance's death in July 1927, her stepson, Staskou, showed a keen interest in writing the story of his stepmother's life. He started his research in the late 1920s and, over the next forty years, he struggled not only to complete the manuscript, but also to find a publisher. Consequently his jaundiced views on O Faolain's work expressed his resentment that someone had actually finished and published a biography.

But before O Faolain had even published his book, Staskou heard that Maeve had been approached by a firm of publishers to write a biography of her mother and this came as a great blow to him. He wanted to prevent her undertaking this work at all costs. He strongly felt that his would be a more competent and sympathetic biography and he seemed to have support from a number of people, including Hanna Sheehy Skeffington and his own father. It appeared that he even wrote direct to Maeve with a view to dissuading her from undertaking the task. He would have felt that Maeve's attitude to her mother's republicanism would preclude her from writing an objective biography.

The matter dragged on. In the end, Mrs Sheehy Skeffington's intervention seemed to finally put Maeve off and she dropped her proposal almost as quickly as she had taken it up. Unfortunately for Staskou, his own endeavours to find a publisher came to nothing and, as his manuscripts have never been found, it is a matter of speculation whether or not he ever did complete a biography or find a publisher.

The death of Casimir Markievicz

After the death of Constance in July 1927, Casimir spent a few quiet days with his old friends in Dublin and then returned to his home in Warsaw. For a number of years before his wife died, Casi had spent very little time in the Irish capital. The thrill of his involvement in the foundling theatres had dimmed; the challenge of writing plays had evaporated and the magic of the bohemian life style he had loved so much in his first days in Ireland had long since disappeared.

There was nothing to keep him in Ireland for the Irish side of the family had drifted into oblivion now that Constance was dead and Maeve was already in England. The Gore-Booths had returned to Lissadell after the death of their notorious Constance and breathed a sigh of relief that the Markievicz episode was over. Staskou alone remained constant to his father. He himself spent time with his father in Warsaw in the days after his stepmother's death although he reappeared in Dublin in the succeeding years.

By the beginning of 1932 Casi was in poor health. He was 58 years old and suffering from heart attacks which greatly debilitated him. Staskou was concerned for his father and was advised to tell Maeve of her father's precarious state of health. At that time relations between Staskou and Maeve were decidedly cool but he realised that, although Maeve had a somewhat condescending attitude to her father, he was her father nonetheless.

Friends and family supported his view of the absolute necessity of telling Maeve and she was informed soon afterwards. Although she did not go to Poland to visit Casi, she did communicate with him. One can only speculate at the contents and sentiments expressed in that communication as it is clear that Maeve was not in the habit of corresponding with her father and therefore was unlikely to be able to express herself as a dutiful and loving daughter. But she had, at least, made contact with her ailing father.

A telegram on 2 December 1932 coldly announced the death of Casimir Dunin de Markievicz. He had died aged 58, just a year younger than Constance had been at the time of her death in 1927. The Irish family were informed that Casimir had died and Maeve sent her condolences to her own Polish relations.

The scattered Markievicz family now constituted just the two children and they showed little likelihood of reconciling. For many years contact between Staskou and Maeve had been tenuous and infrequent. However there were still occasional letters between the two as Staskou continued to struggle with his biography of Constance.

He invited Maeve to come to visit her Markievicz relatives in Poland in the mid 1930s. To ensure that she would have a companion on the journey he also invited Maeve's friend and second cousin, Stella L'Estrange, the girl who had shared her governess with her when they were children at Ardeevin. As the two young women considered this offer of Polish hospitality, Maeve unexpectedly decided that she did not want to go. She gave no real reason for her decision but left it up to Stella as to whether or not she would go alone.

Stella had been greatly looking forward to the visit and so made up her mind to go. She went off on her own and had a wonderful time in Poland - in Warsaw, Kracow and the Tatra Mountains - returning home after some weeks in that lovely country with a diary written to enable her to relive the holiday of a lifetime. Staskou was naturally disappointed that his sister had not wished to visit with her Markievicz relations although he did not find her decision altogether surprising.

During the 1920s, Staskou had been in regular employment in his homeland. The 1930s were bad years throughout the western world and the situation was no different in either Poland or Ireland. By the autumn of 1935, Staskou had decided to return to live in Dublin. Life in Poland had been too much a series of 'ups and downs' and of employment followed by bouts of joblessness. It was time to try his luck in Ireland.

He considered that his best chances would now be in his adopted homeland. He still had no luck in finding a publisher for his book but hoped that, by returning to Ireland, the situation might change. He could not find employment, although shortly after he had arrived in Dublin he had broadcast a number of talks on the radio which had brought him some much needed income.

He lived, somewhat unsatisfactorily, in a succession of 'digs' in Dublin which clearly epitomised his unremitting poverty and impecuniousness. By the beginning of the 'Emergency' (World War Two) in the Free State, however, Staskou had been successful in finding a job as a 'superior canvasser' and was pleased to have landed such a well paid job. But he was now living in yet another lodging and this time with 18 other people and his lifestyle and quality of life had hit an all-time low. He lived in the hope that he could finish his biography; but it seems he never did.

The disastrous world conflict

For the Gore-Booths, life during World War Two consisted of one tragedy after another. Like so many of the gentry families remaining in Ireland, their sons and heirs had enlisted in the forces of the British crown as their ancestors had done for generations past. And, as in previous conflicts, these families had sacrificed their sons in far greater proportion than any other families in the service of the Allied cause. Many Irish families were almost decimated, in many cases leaving no heirs to inherit titles and properties.

In the early days of the war three of the four Gore-Booth sons, Hugh, Brian and Angus, volunteered for duty. Michael, the eldest son, was suffering from the early symptoms of what was to become a debilitating mental illness and he was, therefore, not fit to enlist. Had he been able, he doubtless would have joined up like all his younger brothers. There had been, of course, absolutely no need for this selfless action since they were living in the neutral Irish Free State but there never seemed to be any doubt that these young men would offer their service in the cause of freedom in the Allied cause.

Hugh Gore-Booth, who was born on 6 June 1910, had graduated from Oxford University as a Master of Arts and was a lecturer there in estate management when the war broke out. He opted for the Army on his enlistment and joined the Royal Irish Fusiliers in 1939. He rose to the rank of lieutenant and was once mentioned in dispatches. Whilst on service with his regiment on the Greek island of Leros in the Aegean Sea in November 1943, he fell in action there and was posted as missing. His death was not confirmed until early March 1944. Shortly after receiving this news his father, Sir Josslyn, died at Lissadell on 14 March, aged 75.

Brian Gore-Booth joined the Royal Navy as soon as hostilities commenced in September 1939. He was born on 23 December 1912 and educated at Dartmouth. On leaving school he became a literary agent in London and was making a successful career for himself. He joined HMS Exmouth, a 1,745 ton destroyer, as a sub lieutenant and was an early casualty of the war. His ship was sunk, with all hands, in January 1940, just as the war was in its earliest days. Brian was just 27 years old.

Angus Gore-Booth, born on 25 June 1920, joined the Irish Guards and was promoted to the rank of captain. Although he survived the conflict he suffered from the effects of six long years of combat and was never again a man of robust health. After succeeding to the baronetcy in 1987, he died at Lissadell on 26 January 1996, aged 75.

The sacrifices of the Gore-Booths were high, although another titled family, who lived not so far away, also lost two of their sons. The Brookes of Colebrooke in County Fermanagh (Sir Basil Brooke was Prime Minister of Northern Ireland from 1943 until 1963) had three sons, two of whom were killed in the war with their third son left severely injured.

Back at Lissadell, when the war was over, Lady Gore-Booth had little to celebrate. She had lost her third son in 1940, her second son in 1943 and her husband in 1944. Her youngest son, although he did survive the war, was soon to embark on a short-lived marriage in 1948 which was to end in divorce in 1954. He did, however, produce the only two children (Eirenice and Josslyn) of the entire family of eight.

And saddest of all for the matriarch was the fact that her eldest son and the heir to the Gore-Booth title, Michael, was soon to be committed to a nursing home in England suffering from an increasingly incurable psychiatric disorder. He was to survive as the absent master of Lissadell until his death in 1987.

Lady Gore-Booth's four daughters, Bridget, Rosaleen, Aideen and Gabrielle remained unmarried and the two who remained at home, Gabrielle and Aideen, struggled for many years to keep the Lissadell estate in Gore-Booth hands. Rosaleen and Bridget had long since left home to work as nannies in Northern Ireland.

In Lissadell church, the fallen sons of Lissadell were not forgotten and, situated in the north aisle of the church, are two exquisite stained glass windows by the renowned artist Kitty O'Brien, from An Tur Gloine - the Tower of Glass - in Dublin, entitled 'Courage' and 'Love'. The windows were dedicated in 1949. Beneath the windows on the wall of the aisle, is a beautifully intricate mosaic memorial to Hugh and Brian. Well might Lady Gore-Booth have said of her two lost sons - 'dulce et decorum est pro patria mori' - it is a sweet and honourable thing to die for one's country.

Maeve's wartime contribution

In the weeks before the outbreak of war, Maeve involved herself in making life easier for the Canadian airmen who were billeted in Egerton and she arranged a number of concert parties for them. They greatly appreciated Miss de Markievicz's endeavours and these events allowed them to settle down before having to leave England to enter the theatre of war.

But, as the war clouds continued to gather over Europe, Maeve, somewhat uncharacteristically, suddenly became anxious and nervous. For such a consummately confident person in the eyes of the Egerton villagers, it therefore came as a great surprise to them to hear that Miss de Markievicz had sold Verrall's Oak and was preparing to move away from the comfortable surroundings which had been her home for more than a decade.

In the very first weeks of the conflict, in September 1939, Maeve approached her friends at Oliver's garage in Egerton and asked them to move her belongings to Suffolk. One of the Oliver men agreed to take her but, at the last moment, he was unable to undertake the task. The job of removing Miss de Markievicz and her goods and chattels fell, therefore, to the 17 year old Janet Dawson who, as it transpired, had only three weeks previously passed her driving test.

Janet took the garage's modest Jowett van to Verrall's Oak and there the vehicle was filled to the brim with Maeve's most treasured possessions. The vast majority of furniture and other household items were left at the house. The little van was extremely overloaded which made the business of driving it in wartime conditions, without road signs and lights all the way to Suffolk, a hair-raising feat for the inexperienced, but plucky, Janet.

Maeve was moving on her own for Edith Keable, her former companion, had by now disappeared from the scene. As the two travelled through the Kent and Essex countryside, Janet was regularly requested to stop in almost every village at the local hostelry. On each occasion, Janet remained in the van, whilst Maeve fortified herself in order to continue the journey.

As they sat beside one another in the cab, Maeve poured out her innermost thoughts to a young woman whom she did not know very well. She had become more and more concerned about the state of Europe. She had seen the lamentable outcome of Prime Minister Chamberlain's abortive talks with Adolf Hitler in 1938. She had become obsessed that people in

Egerton would reject her on account of her late mother's nationalist politics which had led to the ignominious withdrawal of the British from Ireland in the early 1920s. She had feared the imminent invasion by the Germans into Kent, the nearest county to the mainland continent of Europe. She may even have feared the prospect of her being interned and considered herself as a 'marked woman'.

And so Maeve de Markievicz, the genial and eccentric lady of Egerton, unexpectedly cut and ran from her haven in the apple orchards of rural Kent. To Janet, Miss de Markievicz was kind and well-meaning yet evidently unhappy. Maeve had been grateful for the young woman's resolve in taking her to Suffolk. However, on arrival at a very pleasant house in the village of Hasketon, near Ipswich, Janet, having helped to unload the van, was then sent on her way by Maeve to make her own way home without even so much as a meal or the offer of a night's stay.

Janet was not at all fazed by Maeve's apparent insensitivity and set out on her journey home. This was rudely interrupted near Colchester by an enemy air raid and she had to find accommodation in trying circumstances as the blackout prevented her from going any further. This she found with a kindly local couple and she returned to Egerton the next day. This episode has remained clear in Janet Oliver's (as she is today) memory even although it took place over 60 years ago.

Maeve then answered the call of king and country and joined the Women's Land Army, as recruit number 14873, later in September 1939. She had much expertise in working on the land, having trained at Swanley and run her business in Egerton, and felt that her talents would be best directed to assisting Britain in her ongoing struggle to feed her people.

She served for part of her service with the Land Army as a welfare officer concerned with the problems of young city girls who had come to the country to work and who found the separation from their homes difficult to bear. The Land Army eventually had over 90,000 young women working on the land producing the food to feed the nation. The young men who had previously been the farmers and farmhands had been called up and it was time for the womenfolk to step in.

Early in 1940, Maeve even returned to Egerton where she worked on the Alexander family's Field Farm and was able to renew some of her old friendships with the local people. She worked hard in the Land Army but decided to leave to take up duties as a fire watcher in early July 1940. London was being heavily blitzed by the Luftwaffe at that time and Maeve did her best in this voluntary work.

At the beginning of the war Maeve renewed her friendship with Penelope Kirby whom she had originally met at Swanley College back in the early 1920s. They were both employed at Swanley once more in 1942 where they became gardening instructors. But Maeve's stay at Swanley was short-lived and she left there again in 1943.

Although Maeve had kept in touch with many of her Irish friends when she lived at Verrall's Oak, she soon began to lose touch even with such good friends as Stella L'Estrange as the war progressed. Friends scattered during the war as they suddenly had to concentrate on life and death matters concerning the greater nation. After the war, however, Maeve and Stella met up again and renewed their lifelong friendship.

8

Life after the War

When the Second World War was finally over, life for Maeve was full of deprivations - just as it was for the rest of the population. She was now living at Parliament Hill with Penelope Kirby. Her regular allowance from the family was now being sent to her by her uncle Mordaunt who had taken over the family responsibilities since his brother, Sir Josslyn's, death in 1944.

Mordaunt did not, however, live at Lissadell but in Oxfordshire. He saw Maeve regularly but was soon exasperated with Maeve on account of her financial frailties.

Around that same time, she was admitted to a rehabilitation unit for those suffering from illnesses attributed to alcohol. The unit was in Chertsey in Surrey and Maeve remained there for a year. Her prognosis was adjudged to be poor but she confounded her critics and was discharged a year later - never to drink again.

Whilst a patient in Chertsey, Maeve was one of the gardeners and was visited regularly by Mordaunt. The debts she had accumulated in Ireland were being cleared up, much to her own and Mordaunt's relief. Although she always publicly denied that she had never returned to Ireland since her mother's death in 1927, Maeve did in fact visit on a few occasions, staying at Lissadell with the Gore-Booths.

30 Parliament Hill, Maeve's London home from mid 1940s to 1962

Maeve now returned to the profession which she knew best - gardening. She was in great need once more of a regular income of her own. She advertised for gardening commissions in the London newspapers and was soon working as a gardener-consultant. Many of the fine gardens in the capital had run wild during the war with no one around to care for them. Maeve gained quite a reputation for her not inconsiderable talent in restoring these wildernesses but woe betide any of her clients who dared to challenge her plans. She knew what was needed in every circumstance and did not countenance interference. But she rarely, if ever, had any dissatisfied customers. Their gardens had been transformed once more thanks to the skill and hard work of this extraordinary woman. Maeve became a well-known eccentric character in the area typified by the Wellington boots and shabby coats which she habitually wore.

For a significant part of her working life, Maeve Markievicz had worked with her hands in the garden. She was accomplished at her work but, as she reached her middle fifties, she quite suddenly diverted from this course and career.

She decided to try her hand at painting. Both her parents had, of course, been accomplished and relatively well known artists - after all they had met one another as they pursued their artistic ambitions in Paris at the turn of the century. Perhaps something creative stirred in Maeve to make this sudden move and she wasted no time in pursuing her new found interest.

As a child at Ardeevin Maeve had once been keen on painting and had pestered anyone and everyone to sit for their 'portraits'. Mary L'Estrange recalled that, when she was just a little girl of five or six, she reluctantly accepted Maeve's invitation to have her portrait painted and, after considerable time and patience, she discovered that the finished painting proved to be a very great disappointment to both artist and sitter alike. According to Mary, Maeve tended to take notions and her painting fad soon gave way to another.

From gardening to painting

However, when she took up her brushes and easel in the mid 1950s, Maeve began to make a success of her new career. She was in her element painting scenes of the beautiful landscapes which were in abundance in and around that part of county Sligo. Over the last years of her life Maeve spent much of her time back in Ireland at Lissadell. She had mellowed with age and her strong dislike for the country had faded.

She painted many local scenes as if to impress them in her memory. 'For as with her mother, however much they rebelled against the Lissadell tradition, Lissadell always remained their spiritual home'.[1] Maeve used oils as her chief medium and she no longer attempted portraits. Her childhood disappointments in this genre had been remembered and were not pursued. She immersed herself in her art bringing the hills and lakes alive on her canvasses. So successful was she that a number of painting exhibitions displaying her works were soon mounted.

She was ambitious for herself and her first exhibition, in April 1959, entitled 'Oil Paintings by Maeve de Markievicz' was held in the High Hill Book Shop in High Street, Hampstead close to her London home. In this part of the capital artists were 'two a penny' and Maeve's decision to exhibit there demonstrated her supreme confidence in the quality of her work.

In his introduction to the artist in the catalogue for the showings the art critic, Kenneth Green, aptly described the life and ambitions of Maeve.

A lively family background, of which her father was Polish and her mother the famous Irish patriot seems to have given Maeve de Markievicz her outspoken and decidedly refreshing character. Failing early to prove herself a violinist, she decided to absorb her creative energies in the making and tending of gardens as a profession. This had been her successful career until one day, two years ago, by then in her middle fifties, she felt an unreasoning and irresistible desire to try to paint a picture. Trembling with excitement, near discouragement as she admits, she made her first tentative essays in landscape. Oils, not watercolours, beguiled her from the outset; also a good idea was first to please herself. Quickly emboldened, Maeve de Markievicz broadened her palette range and was spurred on to a sense of organising her pictures. Rarely painting direct from nature, developing rough pencil notes or pure visual memory or simply inventing, she produced in spare hours from her gardens, a series of canvasses notable for their breadth of handling and vivid outlook...Maeve de Markievicz paints as a real painter, enjoying colour and textual possibilities, exploring and trying to keep the freshness of her medium. In this way, her work is not so much primitive as in keeping with her character, candid and refreshing. We should expect the first exhibition to lead her on to still more interesting and original successes.

This description of Maeve would have greatly pleased her. The critique was read by many of the art critics of the day and an exhibition, even here in Hampstead, was a creditable launch pad for her new found profession. Green's words were decidedly flowery and he doubtless gilded the lily about Maeve's life and her abilities, but he was positive and encouraging in what he had said. Maeve sold a number of her canvasses during this three week show.

However the exhibition which gave Maeve the greatest thrill and the most pleasure was one held in the Old Council Chamber in Sligo Town Hall from 26 June until 7 July 1959. The artists on show were local county Sligo artists, including a number of paintings by Jack and John Yeats. Although Maeve had just one canvas on display - 'Knocknarea from Lissadell' - she realised that she was now exhibiting with Ireland's best known and world famous artists.

Also on display were two works by her father, Casimir, and five by her mother, Constance. Her cousins Bridget and Rosaleen also had paintings hanging in the exhibition. There were paintings by Sir Joshua Reynolds, Percy French and George Russell (AE) also on display. The local newspapers and the Dublin art critics gave generous and appreciative coverage to the exhibition and they noted the work of the newest of the artists on display - Maeve de Markievicz. Maeve had every reason to feel proud of her achievements thus far.

In August 1960 Maeve's first Dublin exhibition, declared open by the Taoiseach, Mr Sean Lemass, was held in the gallery of the prestigious store of Brown Thomas. She had received a great deal of help in setting up this exhibition from one of her mother's original Fianna scouts, Eamon Martin, who had considered it a privilege to be of assistance to the daughter of his childhood heroine, Constance Markievicz, almost exactly fifty years after the formation of the Fianna organisation.

There she sold a number of her paintings and she looked forward to further exhibitions to promote her work. It was at the end of this exhibition as Maeve was soaking up the atmosphere in the stillness of the gallery that an elderly woman approached her to say that she had known her mother, Constance. 'Madame was a beautiful woman, but you are not'. This remark disturbed Maeve but, within a few minutes, the old woman returned with a large bouquet of flowers with the words - 'For Madame's daughter' - and Maeve's faith in humanity had been restored. Had the old lady only paused for a moment she would have seen the likeness between Maeve and her mother in the same fine bone structure and aristocratic bearing of both women. Constance's memory had certainly not been totally forgotten.

Her painting gave her a great deal of pleasure. One of Maeve's seascape paintings is now in the possession of Mary L'Estrange. It had been given by Maeve to Stella L'Estrange as a gift after one of the 1959 exhibitions. It is a pleasant oil on canvas painting in subtle shades of blue, entitled 'Rosses Point, Co. Sligo, Yeats Country' and is signed on the obverse side - 'To Stella L'Estrange from the artist Maeve de Markievicz, September 1961'.

The delight in new friendships

Maeve had a long and serious illness at her London home in the autumn of 1961 and, after she had recovered sufficiently, she made a conscious decision to return to Ireland to continue her painting. 'If I'm going to paint again, I need to return to Sligo'.

By this time, Maeve had met Jim McGarry who lived in Collooney, not far from Sligo town. He had attended the Irish artists' exhibition in Sligo in 1959 and had followed, with interest, the career of this daughter of Constance Markievicz about whom he had heard so many stories when he was a child. He was so impressed with Maeve's paintings that, as a well known local author himself, he decided to write an article for a Sunday newspaper in February 1962 to bring Maeve's life story into the public eye.

In his detailed and comprehensive review, Jim described Maeve's life from her days at home with her grandmother to her schooling, through to her interest and career in gardening to her new found love of painting. He sent Maeve a copy of the newspaper cutting and she immediately replied thanking him for arranging for its publication. On the whole she considered that the article was excellent although she thought that the heading about her inheriting her mother's charm was too complimentary. She insisted that her mother had always much more charm than she had.

Jim then commissioned a work from Maeve to paint Collooney church for his sister. He had specified that the local college was not to feature in the painting and so Maeve complied by depicting the church on the horizon with fields of hay and lapcocks drawing the eye up to the church. Maeve agreed a price of eight guineas, but, in the end, it appeared that Jim's sister did not like the painting.

However 'Collooney Church' by Maeve de Markievicz remains today in the possession of Jim McGarry. Jim and Maeve became friends and he was able to find other clients for her paintings, including the county court judge Naylon, whom she simply called 'the Judge', who bought a

'Collooney Church' by Maeve de Markievicz

number of her works. Another friend was Nora Niland who was known as 'Lady G'. She was the chief librarian in Sligo and she, too, was soon in possession of some of Maeve's paintings. Maeve also hoped that 'Lady G' would be able to arrange for some of her paintings to be exhibited for sale in the library and in other locations for rich American tourists to buy.

In her regular correspondence with Jim McGarry, Maeve frequently remarked at how happy she was to be able to make so many new friends at her age. She was looking forward to spending time back in Ireland at Lissadell in the summer of 1962 although, in her letter to Jim McGarry in May, it began to look as if the Gore-Booths might not be able to put her up.

The death of Maeve de Markievicz

Following her serious illness in 1961, Maeve had been invited to Lissadell for the Christmas break and gladly travelled there to recuperate. This was also an opportunity to renew old friendships. Little did she guess that this Christmas visit would be her last. As she feverishly painted many of the well known haunts of her childhood, Maeve immersed herself in her favourite places, like Cloonagh, a delightful spot which had been immortalised by her aunt Eva in her painting entitled 'The Little Waves of Breffny'. Now Maeve set about painting the scene, but in an altogether different mode. She called her work 'The Angry Waves of Breffny'.

Both at her Christmas break and during her visits in the first months of 1962, Maeve enjoyed meeting her new friends whilst also spending time with some of the older residents of the area listening to stories of her mother's ebullient childhood. One old man recalled the story of Constance and Major O'Hara racing hard to a finish at the Claragh point-to-point races. As they both approached the winning post they were locked together with a dead heat seemingly the most likely result. But, just as the horses rushed to the line, Constance's mount nosed slightly in front and she flashed past the post in first place.

However, before she could pull her horse to a halt, it collapsed on the ground. Constance immediately sat down in the mud and took the horse's head on her lap. She called for whiskey for the beast and, after administering it with due love and attention, she waited patiently until the horse was revived. She cared little for the state of her riding clothes, for she was more concerned that her horse would get back onto its feet. Then, and only then, did she set off for home to change her riding attire.

On another occasion Constance was one of four competitors racing towards the finish line. The other three riders were men who fully expected the young lady rider to give way. But they had not reckoned on Constance's determination as she spurred her mount close to the last fence and across the line, leaving her torn green skirt atop the fence post!

Her last visit to Sligo gave Maeve much pleasure and, as she left to return to her London home, she took a final detour to look at the lovely Ox mountains which can be seen from Lissadell. It was almost as if she knew she would never see these wonderful places again. This little poem which she had written in February 1962 seemed a fitting epitaph:

There is a colour on Benbulben
Indigo on Knocknarea
Gold and grey and primroses
In Lissadell today.

There is fire on Ben Weskin
Ice blue on Sligo Bay
God give us peace and hope
In Lissadell today.

She arrived home in Hampstead to see her companion, Penelope Kirby, but during the evening of 7 June 1962 she became unwell and Penelope called the doctor. Her own general practitioner was not available and the visiting doctor, after examining Maeve, simply prescribed a sleeping pill.

However, during the night, her condition suddenly deteriorated and, before the doctor could return, Maeve had become unconscious and died. On her death certificate, the cause was given as a heart attack following a coronary thrombosis. The date was 8 June 1962; she was just 60 years old. In her will, she had donated her body to medical research and there was, consequently, no burial service. Neither was there any memorial service. She left all her worldly goods, such as they were, to Penelope Kirby.

The *Irish News* of 11 June 1962 carried this obituary, recording the unexpected passing of the daughter of Constance Markievicz.

> The death occurred suddenly in London on Friday of Miss Maeve Markievicz, daughter of Countess Markievicz.
>
> Maeve Markievicz, who was an artist, was born at Lissadell House, county Sligo about 60 years ago. She was educated in England and lived in Sligo until the death of her grandmother, Lady Gore-Booth, in 1926 after which she went to live in England. During her time there, she was a landscape gardener and, on the outbreak of the last war, she was a welfare officer in the Land Army.
>
> She took up painting late in her life as 'a hobby for my old age'. She was successful and held many exhibitions in Hampstead, London, where she lived.
>
> She exhibited in Dublin some time ago when the Taoiseach, Mr Sean Lemass, performed the opening ceremony.
>
> Her death took place at 30 Parliament Hill, London NW3 where she lived with her lifelong friend, Miss Kirby. She was with her when she died. She lived there for over 20 years.

Although this newspaper fairly accurately reported the details of Maeve's passing, there were some mistakes. They did not seem sure of her exact age; they got the date of Lady Gore-Booth's death wrong and they did not take the trouble to find out Miss Kirby's first name.

But they had done their job and, for anyone interested in Dublin and throughout the Republic of Ireland, they had faithfully informed its readers of the death of the only child of one of the country's most honoured daughters, Constance Markievicz. It had been some time since her name had been mentioned in the press and the fact that her daughter had now died, concluded the final chapter in the life of an Irish heroine. Few Irishmen and women would even have remembered that Maeve had existed and many would have expressed surprise when they read the obituary.

Just over twelve months later, on 5 October 1963, another newspaper report, this time in the *Sligo Champion*, drew the attention of its readers with the following headline.

Memorial Tablet Unveiled

A memorial tablet to Maeve, the only child of Constance, Countess Markievicz, was unveiled at Lissadell church by the Bishop of Kilmore.

A moving panegyric was delivered by His Lordship to a large congregation of all religious creeds and classes.

Many of the older members of the congregation remembered Maeve and her mother with great affection. They felt too, as does His Lordship, that both women possessed alike many of their outstanding qualities, in particular that of great humanity which manifested itself in their daily actions.

The many friends of Maeve who travelled to this simple yet moving ceremony were entertained later by Lady Gore-Booth at Lissadell House in a manner that would have pleased both Madame and her daughter, Maeve.

The inscription on the memorial tablet reads "To the Glory of God, in loving memory of Maeve Alys Dunin-Markievicz, November 13, 1901 - June 8, 1962, daughter of Constance Georgine and Casimir Dunin-Markievicz. Inasmuch as you have done it unto one of the least of my brethren, you have done it unto me".

The words of Bishop Edward Moore at this service rang hollow. These two women may not have been remembered with any true affection in the area, although many would have respected Constance for the stance that she had taken in the fight for a free Ireland. There certainly would also have been many who saw her as nothing short of a traitor.

And as 'for the many friends of Maeve', one wonders who these people were. Maeve had severed her links with Sligo after the death of her grandmother, although it would be fair to say that she had at least returned to paint in the area in her last years and had made a number of new friends and renewed old acquaintances.

It must have been difficult for the bishop to strike a balance in his 'panegyric' for he realised that Lady Gore-Booth, the chief mourner - and now an elderly lady of 78 - would not have wanted any degree of coldness or contention to creep into the words that he had chosen to say to those gathered at Lissadell church that day. The people who had attended the church service would have had their own memories of these extraordinary women as they sipped tea in the grand salons of Lissadell House that October afternoon.

That memorial tablet to Maeve is situated on the north wall of the church opposite the entrance door. It is the largest wall tablet but it is now, 40 years after its erection and dedication, becoming sadly discoloured. Some of the lettering suffers from the effects of poor workmanship and has begun to fade. This final remembrance of the daughter of Ireland's 'Joan of Arc' offers an inadequate memorial to a woman whose life could well have been absolutely forgotten.

Memorial tablet in Lissadell Parish Church

9

The Bond between Maeve and Constance

No one can argue that Maeve and Constance Markievicz led bizarre and unconventional lives, both in their relationship as mother and daughter and as individuals. Ireland's historians have largely forgotten Maeve and have tended to underestimate and neglect Constance and the contribution that she made to the New Ireland.

The important role played by Lady Gore-Booth, Maeve's grandmother, must be seen as the pivotal relationship in each of their lives. Georgina, Lady Gore-Booth was the archetypal wife and mother of the Big House at Lissadell. She married Sir Henry and had five children including, most importantly, an heir. She tolerated her husband's long absences when he was away from home for lengthy spells exploring the Arctic regions. She worried about him, and with justification. There were many occasions when his life was in danger and the likelihood of their young son, Josslyn, being catapulted into the position of master at Lissadell was constantly a distinct possibility.

She always took time to attend to the needs of her tenants and was, without doubt, the much loved lady of the manor. She supported her husband in his various endeavours at Lissadell, including sharing in his interest in horticulture and botany. She greatly loved and admired her husband and she was by his side in his last illness when they travelled to Switzerland to seek a cure, albeit unsuccessfully, for his ailments.

That generation of Gore-Booths also naturally looked to a smooth transition to the next. It was expected that the son and heir would marry and take on the responsibilities of running Lissadell. It was hoped that their three daughters would find themselves suitable husbands with whom to settle down. It was expected that Lady Gore-Booth, by the early years of the twentieth century, would be able to live out the remainder of her life in a dignified and restful widowhood.

But things were not to work out for her as she could have reasonably expected. Her son, Josslyn, did not marry for seven years after his father's death although, in the end, he and his wife did have eight children. Her younger son also married and had two sons, although he had decided to spend his adult life in England.

Her second daughter, Eva, was to prove somewhat of an anomaly for Lady Gore-Booth. To have a child interested in the needs of the poor in Manchester, and a poet too, was not exactly what she had expected of such an intelligent girl. As far as her third daughter, Mabel, was concerned everything did work out well for she married an eminently eligible young man and went off to his English home to care for the two children of their marriage.

However Lady Gore-Booth's firstborn, and her first daughter, was a child with whom no one could ever have reckoned. Constance was destined to lead a most eventful and exciting life. It was certainly not the kind of life that her mother would have ever anticipated - even in her wildest dreams or darkest nightmares.

Constance proved to be an outlandish child. She did not conform to the rules of the house. She made life difficult for her parents and her governess and for anyone around her. She was strong-willed and hard to discipline. She was often found in some far flung corner of the estate talking to the workmen, helping the tenant women in the care of their children or simply galloping around on horseback.

None of these attributes were, of themselves, unusually intractable but they did cause growing concerns for her parents. They knew, from early on, that she would not be a conformer, and this proved to be the case. Constance tended to a rude child and quite prepared to answer back to her elders. This made her popular with the tenants who saw their 'Miss Gore' as the headstrong daughter of their Big House. They enjoyed seeing her gallop on horseback and leading the hunt in the fox chase far ahead of her adult companions. It was fun to see this fine young woman trounce the other horsemen and women by outmanoeuvring them and winning race after race.

Rebel or individualist?

Constance was not a rebel; rather she was an individualist who set her own rules and who chose to ignore the time honoured customs of her class. In many ways, consequently, Constance could have been seen as a disappointment to her mother. After her marriage to Casimir even her own maternal ties to her daughter, Maeve, were to be stretched unmercifully throughout their entire lives.

In the last decade of the nineteenth century, when Constance was in her twenties, Sir Henry and his wife looked in vain for a suitable partner for their daughter. Once it had seemed possible that they had succeeded in their endeavours when Constance met a young man called Philip Percival but nothing came of this relationship and he soon emigrated to Australia.

In the end she managed to browbeat her parents into allowing her to study art at the Slade in London and, for her parents, there seemed nothing more they could do, even though they kept her allowance to a minimum in a desperate attempt that she might then conform.

They soon lost their daughter to a bohemian lifestyle more in keeping with the offspring of the artisan classes. When their daughter moved on to study in Paris amidst its seedy cafes on the Left Bank and its dingy ateliers and studios, they felt that their links with their unconventional daughter had been irretrievably disrupted.

They then heard of Constance's romance with a foreign nobleman with an unpronounceable name and, when they discovered that this flirtation was likely to end in marriage, they shuddered at the prospect of such a union. With heavy hearts, the Gore-Booths submitted to their daughter's request that she marry her Casimir Markievicz. It would have been pointless and churlish to withhold their blessing.

As so often happened in the chequered history of the Gore-Booth family of Lissadell, fate intervened. Sir Henry had died in the early days of 1900. Constance, for all her bravado and nonconformity, grieved at the loss of her father. She consoled her mother and, in order not to further upset her feelings, the family agreed that the marriage of Constance and Casi would take place quietly in September 1900. Lady Gore-Booth returned to Lissadell after the London wedding in a solemn mood. She wondered what would become of her daughter and this union with her Polish husband.

Then, just over a year later, the couple had their one and only child, their daughter Maeve. The child's birth was to have a profound effect on the lives of three people - the child's mother, the child's grandmother and the child herself.

An unconventional upbringing

Most wondered how Constance would deal with a child of her own. Many theories have been proffered about this provocative notion and countless differing points of view expounded. It has always been common currency to proclaim that Maeve was simply abandoned by her mother; that Constance had no time for her own child and that she was well rid of her. The mention of Maeve's name in biographies of her mother speak of the fact that Lady Gore-Booth was willing and able to take over the upbringing of her granddaughter when she saw that her own single-minded daughter had little intention of being an attentive parent to her child.

Neither had the child's father, Casi, much time for Maeve. He was much too interested in the artistic and theatrical life in Dublin to be concerned with Maeve. And he had a son too - Stanislaus, known as Staskou. Relations with his own son, especially in the early days in Dublin, were patchy at best although they were to improve later in their lives.

Lady Gore-Booth's attitude to the upbringing of Maeve was very positive. When Maeve was born at Lissadell in November 1901, she was her first grandchild. Mabel's children, John and Moira, were born relatively soon afterwards but they lived at their own home in England.

And so Maeve became the centre of attention. At the outset she was left with her grandmother although she did spend some time during the five years from 1903 until 1908 in Dublin with her bohemian parents. Significantly the vital and formative first two years of her life were spent with Lady Gore-Booth. She was able to mould the little girl and helped to prepare her to cope with those few chaotic years she was to spend at her parents' home at St Mary's, Rathgar. When Maeve eventually returned to Ardeevin in 1908, she was to remain in her grandmother's custody for the rest of Lady Gore-Booth's life. It was at this point that the relationship between Constance and Maeve bgean to waver.

Firstly Maeve had to be settled down when she returned to Sligo, since her days in Dublin had been so undisciplined and disturbing. Constance and Casi had had no time for their children. They were too busy engaging in the social round at the Vice regal court, the theatres and the art galleries of Dublin. Their lives centred around these aspects of social life and definitely not on their children.

To their parents, Maeve and Staskou were somewhat of an encumbrance. In 1908, therefore, Staskou was packed off to school in Gorey and Maeve was recalled to Ardeevin. The Markieviczs no longer had to concern themselves with their two offspring.

Lady Gore-Booth was well into her sixties when Maeve came to live permanently with her. She saw in Maeve another spirited child - in many ways just like her mother - but she was determined to shape her and turn her into a conforming child. She took control of the little girl's life and, in doing so, formed a close bond with her.

Lady Gore-Booth lavished love and attention on Maeve; she employed an able and competent governess to look after her; she ensured that there were a few friends around with whom Maeve could relate and she taught the child exactly what was expected of a Gore-Booth. Attendance at Sunday services at Lissadell church; active involvement with every good cause that was required of the children of the Big House and, above all, the need to exude confidence in her dealings with her peers and with the tenants of the estate. Lady Gore-Booth succeeded in most of these endeavours for Maeve not only became a confident child but also actually turned out to be a precocious and gifted young person.

But most important of all, Lady Gore-Booth managed to become a substitute for her own daughter, Constance, in the affections of Maeve. When Constance did visit Ardeevin after 1908 - although such visits had become more and more irregular - it was clear to her that the maternal link between Maeve and herself was becoming more and more fragile. This did not concern Constance for she was, by now, totally immersed in her nationalist activities in Dublin. She trusted her mother and, in effect, relied on her to provide affection and love which she herself was incapable of giving or simply did not have time to give.

And what of Maeve?

It certainly did not mean that Constance was an unkind and uncaring person, but she saw her life's work in a completely different arena. Her passion for Ireland could never have been tempered by the presence of a child. The needs of Irishmen and women far outweighed not only the needs of Constance but also those of her daughter. Therefore after Constance had reached the age of forty in 1908, her life and very existence became single minded and focussed - not on her daughter and her family life (which by then was largely non existent anyway) - but on the plethora of organisations with which she was deeply and entirely involved.

Let it not be said that she formally abandoned Maeve. She had truthfully neglected her in an emotional way, yet physically she knew her child was in good hands. Very few people, especially women who knew Constance, accepted her reasons for leaving Maeve with her grandmother.

Most Irishwomen saw any mother who did not care for her own child as a disgrace to motherhood and something which could never be excused. The Catholic Church had its own strict views on the bringing up of children and Constance did not conform to these. She was still, of course, not a Roman Catholic herself - although by 1917 she had embraced Catholicism.

Constance had one friend who saw her dilemma. Maud Gonne MacBride, herself a strong-willed woman, declared that 'Constance loved children and it was a great sacrifice when she sent Maeve to be brought up by her mother because life's evolution had made things too strenuous for the child at home. Only people who knew her very closely and intimately knew how deeply she felt, for with her own exuberant manner and frank way of speaking she was very reserved about her personal feelings and kept things deep hidden in her heart'.[1]

This says much about Constance Markievicz. In many ways it proves that she was essentially a lonely woman. Throughout her later years, when she was in prison or 'on the run' or speaking out in opposition to the Treaty in the Dail, she spoke her mind regardless of what people thought of her. Her views were always expressed in a trenchant and uncompromising manner.

There was never any doubt that, when given a job to do, for example when she was de Valera's Minister of Labour, she did it extremely well. She was meticulous and competent, but strangely detached from those around her. She had friends in the women's organisations; she had contacts with the labour leaders, Connolly and Larkin; she worked well with her colleagues in her Ministry or in the St Patrick's constituency which she represented in the Dail.

But Constance relied heavily and almost entirely on her sister, Eva, as a confidante when she endured her many prison sentences. In Aylesbury prison, for instance, she was totally on her own as the only Irish prisoner to be incarcerated there. In her frequent correspondence with Eva, she wrote about her trying circumstances in jail and established an even closer bond with her sister.

As time went on, this tie became much more meaningful to both sisters. It was, to them, a mystical attachment. It drew them closer and closer together. They became exclusive people and, in consequence, others were squeezed out of their thoughts. And the one mainly forgotten was Maeve.

It is true that there was some mention of Maeve in a few of these many letters but there was never any depth to the enquiries. It was a superficial interest about such inconsequential matters as asking her brother to give Maeve money for an Easter egg or some trivial matter over photographs and music lessons. There were few letters from mother to daughter. Constance had long since become disjointed, disillusioned and distant from her one and only child. 'Maeve was estranged in spirit through indoctrination and absence'.[2]

As Maeve grew up at Ardeevin, forging a close relationship not only with her Gaga but also with her once hard-pressed governess, Janet Clayton, she realised that there was never going to be any strong association with her own mother. This position she had accepted and, as a result, Maeve became defensive when thinking or speaking of Constance. She became used to standing on her own feet for she saw less and less of her eccentric mother.

It is strange to relate that Constance, in one of her prison letters, thought that Maeve had been 'amused' by her involvement in the Rising. This was hardly the case. Constance, by 1916, was a well known personality in nationalist Dublin and had become a thorn in the flesh of the British administration. She was no longer the favoured Madame de Markievicz at the Viceregal court and, at home at Lissadell, Constance was a decided embarrassment and discussion about her was frowned upon. To Maeve her mother was now beyond redemption and the less that was spoken of her, the better. She was still at home during the Easter Rising when she heard the fate which was to befall her mother.

Having been sentenced to death for her part in the rebellion, the family was relieved that, on General Maxwell's orders, this was to be commuted to penal servitude. Nonetheless the whole matter had been a great embarrassment for the Gore-Booths. Despite the family's discomfiture, Lady Gore-Booth was able to express her concern for her wayward daughter and she did have compassion for her, although the remainder of her family tried their best to forget the matter.

When Maeve was at school in England, Constance spent the majority of these years in prison or 'on the run'. They did not see one another; they gave little thought to one another; they became yet more estranged.

Maeve's reactions

Being in England during the latter part of the First World War was a relief for Maeve. She did not have to listen to the news of troubles in Ireland and was safely secreted away in Barton Court and then in London.

As far as Constance was concerned, this period was her most challenging time, either being incarcerated or endeavouring to run her Labour department. She revelled in this 'cat and mouse' existence and nothing pleased her more than to successfully evade capture by government agents. In course of time they did catch up with her but she still managed to undertake vast amounts of work for the department for which she had responsibility. Maeve did not feature in her thoughts and, as far as Maeve was concerned, her mother's activities seemed a million miles away and far beyond her care or interest.

Little is known about contacts between Eva and Maeve for there had never been many in the past. Not long after Constance's death in 1927 (by which time Lady Gore-Booth was also dead) Maeve, for some reason best known to herself, deliberately tore up most of the letters which had been sent by Eva to Constance. (Eva, too, was dead by this time).

No reason is given for Maeve acting in this hurtful manner. She may have had a legitimate explanation for this outburst but it certainly must have astonished and distressed those who were present. On account of their lifelong relationship Esther Roper would have desperately wanted to have been given Eva's letters; to see them ripped up practically in her presence would have been hard to bear. It seems that Casi was present during this incident yet took no action to prevent it.

This speaks volumes about Casi and his attitude to his daughter too. He had not seen much of Maeve in recent years and, although they had shown solidarity at the time of Constance's funeral, tensions had quickly surfaced. They may have been father and daughter but, in terms of expressing love and affection for one another, little existed. They were poles apart emotionally and Maeve's reasons for destroying the letters could well have had something to do with the fact that so many had been written by Constance to Eva yet so very few had ever been written to her. Perhaps Maeve had been expressing frustration rather than trying to offend those present.

But the episode left a bitter taste in the mouths of all concerned. It was a revelation to Staskou as well. Hanna Sheehy Skeffington was confirmed in her dislike of Maeve Markievicz after this episode and, although Maeve needed on occasion to correspond with Hanna as she was her mother's executrix, there never was any love lost between these two women.

Another possible reason for the rift between Constance and Maeve was Constance's supposed preference for boys. She may have hoped for a son and was therefore disappointed when Maeve was born. But there are no references - subtle or otherwise - to Constance not loving her daughter for that specific reason.

Her husband, of course, had two sons to his first wife, Jadwiga, before she died. His younger son had also died but Staskou had survived. Constance was entranced when she first met this boy and she danced for joy when she was successful in persuading her mother-in-law to permit Staskou to come to live in Dublin with his father and herself.

Yet there is no evidence that Constance showed extra affection towards Staskou when the family lived together for those five short years at St Mary's, Rathgar from 1903 until 1908. She was as flighty and careless with him as with Maeve. The Markieviczs' friends often remarked at Constance's lack of discipline over her wild children. Many of them considered that Constance was almost neglectful of the way she ran her household in regard to child care.

Constance had her Fianna na hEireann. Of all the achievements in her life, she looked upon her formation of these scouts as her finest hour. At the beginning some of the new scouts had complained about women being involved in the movement but, when they were reminded that the idea had been Constance's, they soon learned to appreciate and cherish her as their Chief Scout.

Her greatest pleasure was to have groups of these boys out at her cottage at Ballally in the Dublin hills. The early stories of her feeble attempts at moulding them together were laughable and the time and money she spent during her short-lived cooperative commune with the Fianna proved how much her heart was in the work of encouraging boys to enjoy themselves.

Whether or not she realised that many of her scouts were secret members of the Irish Republican Brotherhood (IRB) is a matter of conjecture. On balance she probably did know but she decided that it was a reasonable price to pay to continue her love affair with her Boy Scout organisation. This singular contribution to Ireland epitomises exactly what the boys meant to her.

And when she was involving herself in teaching the boys to shoot and to learn camp skills, Maeve was back at Ardeevin, solitary and alone.

She never benefited from any of her mother's apparent enthusiasms for the outdoor life. Maeve found pleasure in caring for horses, learning to play tennis and to being moulded into a graceful young lady and debutante. She knew, too, that her mother always preferred boys and that her enthusiasms were directed towards them. Constance was never even keen on girl 'sluas' (troops) in the Fianna movement.

Life for Constance in Dublin was hectic whereas life for Maeve in Sligo was the exact opposite, quiet and serene. The type of life that Maeve was living was not the frenetic one that her mother had experienced when she was young. Maeve reluctantly accepted that her life was altogether different and thereby separate from her mother's.

A relationship at last

In the end, however, Constance did not entirely abandon Maeve. It was not the classic example of maternal deprivation. It is true that there never had been any quality time for Maeve and Constance as mother and daughter during Maeve's early years but they did meet up with one another reasonably regularly during some of Constance's last years.

Perhaps it could be agreed that theirs was never to be the normal parent-child relationship, even although this realisation only became clear late on. Anne Haverty very succinctly makes the point - 'But although their relationship was often distant and desultory, they were never estranged. It was a relationship more typical of friends than mother and daughter; it conformed to Con's habit of camaraderie and talk of mutual interests in place of intimacy or emotional involvement'.[3]

As adults, they did have time for one another. Maeve, for example, had learned to drive and when Constance needed help to service her ancient Ford motor car, Maeve was often there to come to her aid. Both loved the intricacies of the motor engine and they were in their element when dismantling it to discover its faults and flaws. The Markievicz women had discovered their connection, perhaps not in close physical bonds, but in the inanimate form of a motor car engine.

They were clinically unemotional towards each other and thus found it difficult to express human love for one another. The fact that this revelation came late in Constance's life precluded any lasting and significant pleasure for the two women. But, in a strange way, Constance had been able to make up for some lost time when she was able to meet and spend time with her daughter, as well as with her own mother when they all appeared together in Dublin on occasion.

Lady Gore-Booth, Constance and Maeve spent the summer months of 1925 and 1926 enjoying shopping expeditions to Brown Thomas' store in Grafton Street. There the elderly grandmother, the gaunt and exhausted mother and the pretty and gay young daughter could, at last, laugh and smile and haggle over the price of a skirt or a hat as many other families were accustomed to doing throughout their lives. This opportunity came belatedly but they certainly enjoyed these family outings.

For years this prospect would have seemed highly improbable, if not impossible. They cherished these moments, which so soon were to sadly end with the demise of first the grandmother and then, so shortly and tragically afterwards, the mother. The young woman was then all too suddenly on her own.

Maeve viewed the last days of her mother's life with apprehension as Constance's health gradually deteriorated. Her mother's years in prison and custody had taken their toll and the once vivacious, confident and stunning woman was reduced to living as a lodger in the home of a friend and her family. She had not even a home of her own.

She was to be seen driving to the Dublin hills and filling her old car with peat and other fuel for the poor of the city slums. She struggled up the flights of rickety stairs of the once beautiful and desirable mansions to give practical assistance to the down-and-outs. She had become an angel of mercy, although her efforts were not always appreciated by all of those she sought to help.

Maeve was, by this time, at her college in England. Once more she had become separated from her mother. She did not fully appreciate that her mother, in undertaking her good works, was so seriously damaging her health. Throughout Maeve's own life, there were few examples of her giving the practical assistance to those less well off than herself except, perhaps, in the work she undertook in the Women's Land Army during the Second World War when she did show thoughtfulness and compassion.

In the end, when Constance was fighting for her life at Sir Patrick Dun's hospital, Maeve was again out of touch with her mother. Those relatively recent times out shopping with Constance seemed as far away as ever. When she was urgently summoned to her mother's bedside, Maeve suffered pangs of remorse. However, her mother was delighted to see all her family around her in her death throes.

When she died, Maeve was consumed with guilt. Her virtual separation from her father and Staskou meant that family ties would now be almost completely broken. From this point onwards her main contact was with her uncle Josslyn with only occasional contact with her father and stepbrother.

The place of Constance Markievicz is assured in Ireland's history. There are, however, to this very day, voices of discontent and a lack of charity in the hearts of some Irishmen and women who still find it difficult to accept her contribution to a free Ireland simply because of the background from which she sprang.

In contrast the name of Maeve de Markievicz is either unknown or totally forgotten and yet her life was indelibly linked with that of her notorious mother - the life of the one was inextricably influenced by the life of the other.

Life after Constance

The name of Constance Markievicz, which had been on the lips of everyone in Ireland for two decades, had grown dim. The Free State government was struggling to make progress in an increasingly impoverished world. Unemployment and emigration were Ireland's principal difficulties and Cosgrave's ever more embattled supporters were hoping for an upturn in their fortunes.

However the assassination of their Minister for Justice and External Affairs (and effective leader during Cosgrave's bouts of illness), Kevin O'Higgins, greatly spooked the Cumann na hGaedheal government. And the arrival of Eamon de Valera and his newly formed Fianna Fail party in the Dail, though very belatedly, also meant increasing pressure on Cosgrave to fulfil his election promises.

When Constance died just five days after O'Higgins' assassination, the whole country was in the depths of despair. The contrasts of the two funerals - O'Higgins' and Constance's - could not have been more marked. Kevin O'Higgins was surrounded by top-hatted and morning-suited men at his obsequies whereas Constance was mourned by thousands of the poor, dishevelled women of Dublin who had held 'Madame' in such high esteem.

Maeve returned to England. Her father and stepbrother went back to their native Poland and the rest of the family took up the reins at

Lissadell once more. The whole family regrouped, now without a mother and two sisters. It was a time to reflect on the past twenty years when a sister of Lissadell had been daily news in republican circles in Dublin and throughout Ireland while her daughter had to spend her young life in the company of her grandmother.

Maeve had now reached her point of no return. She would spend most of her next three decades far away from the land of her birth and any contacts were simply by letter and the very occasional visit. Her mother had gone, although she was thankful that she had been somewhat reconciled with Constance in the immediate years prior to her death.

Her attitude to keeping her mother's memory alive defied convention. She did not pursue the offer of a publisher to write a biography of Constance. Maeve had no feel for writing such a biography and Staskou was correct when he said that Maeve knew little of Constance's life and even cared less about it. It came as a relief that Maeve did not attempt such a task.

A biography of Constance Markievicz by her only daughter would have been ill advised. Nor did she help Staskou when she was told that he intended to undertake the same job. He never succeeded in finding a publisher for his book and, although a biography of his could have been a little more objective, the fact that it was never published came as no surprise. Staskou's chequered lifestyle was not conducive to his writing the story either.

When biographies did eventually appear, they were heavily criticised for their lack of real insight into the contribution made by Constance Markievicz to Ireland. It may be, therefore, that no universally acclaimed biography will ever be written.

Maeve went back to England where she remained until the last part of her own life. There she endeavoured to make a name for herself in landscape gardening and then in painting.

Maeve Markievicz had a favoured upbringing. She had the advantage of a doting and loving grandmother. She had the companionship of her two great friends, Edith Keable and Penelope Kirby, for most of her later life. She had little time for men and never married - she found the friendship of women more rewarding and fulfilling than that of men.

Hers could be described as an unfulfilled and sad life. The reason for this could be laid at the feet of her own mother whose conversion to nationalism meant that her only child could never have the family life which she herself had experienced. Nonetheless Maeve impressed those who knew her, especially during the times towards the end of her life when she was painting in county Sligo, as a thoughtful person who had a close affinity with those less well off than she was.

Sadly Maeve Markievicz has left little to posterity - some paintings of mediocre value, a marble memorial in the church at Lissadell and a fading recollection for a very few of those older members of the family and others in England and Sligo who survive today. Yet she was the daughter of a great and revered Irishwoman and, as such, her place in history is assured.

Notes and References

Chapter 1
1. Jim McGarry's unpublished account, 13 June 1962.
2. Sawyer, Roger, *We are but Women* (London 1993) p. 43.
3. *The Irish Worker*, 17 October 1931.
4. Durand, Stella, *Drumcliffe - the Church of Ireland Parish in its North Sligo Setting* (Manorhamilton 2000) pp. 67 & 69.

Chapter 2
1. Jim McGarry's unpublished account, 13 June 1962.
2. *Ibid..*
3. *The Irish Worker*, 17 October 1931.
4. Marreco, Anne, *The Rebel Countess, the Life and Times of Constance Markievicz* (London 1967) p. 97.
5. *The Irish Worker*, 17 October 1931.
6. Sawyer, Roger, *We are but Women* (London 1993) p. 43.
7. Marreco, Anne, *The Rebel Countess, the Life and Times of Constance Markievicz* (London 1967) p. 125.
8. Haverty, Anne, *Constance Markievicz - an Independent Life* (London 1988) p. 52.
9. Van Voris, Jacqueline, *Constance de Markievicz, in the Cause of Ireland* (Amherst, Massachusetts 1967) p. 50.

Chapter 3
1. Bridget Gore-Booth's unpublished note, no date.
2. Marreco, Anne, *The Rebel Countess, the Life and Times of Constance Markievicz* (London 1967) p. 124.
3. Haverty, Anne, *Constance Markievicz - an Independent Life* (London 1988) p. 70.
4. Marreco, Anne, *The Rebel Countess, the Life and Times of Constance Markievicz* (London 1967) p. 125.
5. *Ibid.*, p. 127.

Chapter 4
1. Marreco, Anne, *The Rebel Countess, the Life and Times of Constance Markievicz* (London 1967) p. 52.
2. *Ibid.*, p. 227.
3. Norman, Diana, *Terrible Beauty, a Life of Constance Markievicz* (London 1987) p. 163.
4. *Sligo Independent*, 26 October 1916.
5. *Ibid..*
6. *Ibid..*
7. *Ibid..*
8. *Sligo Champion*, 5 May 1917.

Chapter 5

1. Markievicz, Constance, *Prison Letters* (London 1934) p. 219.
2. *Ibid.*, p. 231.
3. National Library of Ireland, MS 13,778, May 1922.
4. *The Irish Worker*, 17 October 1931.
5. Norman, Diana, *Terrible Beauty, a Life of Constance Markievicz* (London 1987) p. 272.
6. National Library of Ireland, MS 13,778, 14 January 1926.
7. Markievicz, Constance, *Prison Letters* (London 1934) p. 307.
8. Van Voris, Jacqueline, *Constance de Markievicz, in the Cause of Ireland* (Amherst, Massachusetts 1967) p. 345.
9. Norman, Diana, *Terrible Beauty, a Life of Constance Markievicz* (London 1987) p. 276.
10. *The Irish Worker*, 17 October 1931.
11. *Ibid.*.
12. Van Voris, Jacqueline, *Constance de Markievicz, in the Cause of Ireland* (Amherst, Massachusetts 1967) p. 349.

Chapter 6

1. National Library of Ireland, MS 33,606 [17], 6 July 1928.
2. Ibid..
3. Ibid..
4. Rita Lees' article in *The Irish Garden*, July/August 1996 pp. 44 & 45.
5. Doreen Weeks' letter, June 2002.
6. Mary James' letter, June 2002.

Chapter 8

1. Jim McGarry's unpublished account, 13 June 1962.

Chapter 9

1. Haverty, Anne, *Constance Markievicz - an Independent Life* (London 1988) pp. 183 & 184.
2. Marreco, Anne, *The Rebel Countess, the Life and Times of Constance Markievicz* (London 1967) p. 227.
3. Haverty, Anne, *Constance Markievicz - an Independent Life* (London 1988) pp. 52 & 53.

Bibliography

Printed Sources

The National Library - Sheehy Skeffington Papers

Secondary Sources

Books

1. Bence-Jones, Mark, *Twilight of the Ascendancy*, London, 1987.
2. Bromage, Mary, *De Valera and the March of a Nation*, London, 1956.
3. Caulfield, Max, *The Easter Rebellion*, London, 1963.
4. Colum, Padraic, *Arthur Griffith*, Dublin, 1959.
5. Coogan, Tim Pat, *Michael Collins*, London, 1990.
6. Coxhead, Elizabeth, *Daughters of Erin*, London, 1965.
7. Dangerfield, George, *The Damnable Question*, Boston/Toronto, 1976.
8. Dooley, Terence, *The Decline of the Big House in Ireland*, Dublin, 2001.
9. Duff, Charles, *Six days to Shake an Empire*, London, 1966.
10. Durand, Stella, *Drumcliffe - the Church of Ireland Parish in its North Sligo Setting*, Manorhamilton, 2000.
11. Edwards, Anne, *I Bought a Dream*, London, 1960.
12. Egerton Local History Group, *A History of Egerton 1900-2000*, Egerton, Kent, 2001.
13. Foster, R.F., *Modern Ireland - 1600-1972*, London, 1988.
14. Foy, Michael and Barton, Brian, *The Easter Rising*, Stroud, 1999.
15. Greaves, C. Desmond, *The Life and Times of James Connolly*, London, 1961.
16. Holt, Edgar, *Protest in Arms - the Irish Troubles 1916-1923*, London, 1960.
17. Kiberd, Declan (ed.), *1916 - Easter Rebellion Handbook*, Dublin, 1998.
18. Haverty, Anne, *Constance Markievicz - an Independent Life*, London, 1988.
19. Levenson, Leah and Natterstad, Jerry, *Hanna Sheehy-Skeffington - Irish Feminist*, Syracuse, 1986.
20. Levenson, Samuel, *James Connolly, a Biography*, London, 1973.
21. Levenson, Samuel, *A Biography of Yeats' Beloved Maud Gonne*, New York, 1976.

22. Lewis, Gifford, *Eva Gore-Booth and Esther Roper - a Biography*, London, 1988.
23. Luddy, Maria, *Women in Ireland 1800-1918 - a Documentary History*, Cork, 1995.
24. Macardle, Dorothy, *The Irish Republic*, London, 1937.
25. Macbride, Maud Gonne, *A Servant of the Queen*, Gerrards Cross, 1994.
26. Markievicz, Constance, *Prison Letters*, London, 1934.
27. Marreco, Anne, *The Rebel Countess, the Life and Times of Constance Markievicz*, London, 1967.
28. Morrow, Anne, *Picnic in a Foreign Land - the Eccentric Lives of the Anglo-Irish*, London, 1989.
29. Norman, Diana, *Terrible Beauty, a Life of Constance Markievicz*, London, 1987.
30. O'Donovan, Donal, *Kevin Barry and his Time*, Sandycove, 1989.
31. O Faolain, Sean, *Constance Markievicz or the Average Revolutionary*, London, 1934.
32. O'Grady, John, *The Life and Work of Sarah Purser*, Blackrock, 1996.
33. O'Neill, Marie, *From Parnell to de Valera - a Biography of Jennie Wise Power 1858-1941*, Dublin, 1991.
34. O'Rahilly, Aodogan, *Winding the Clock - O'Rahilly and the 1916 Rising*, Dublin, 1991.
35. Sawyer, Roger, *'We are but Women' - Women in Ireland's History*, London, 1993.
36. Van Voris, Jacqueline, *Constance de Markievicz, in the Cause of Ireland*, Amherst, Massachusetts, 1967.
37. Wallace, Martin, *100 Irish Lives*, London, 1983.
38. Ward, Margaret, *Maud Gonne - a Biography*, London, 1990.
39. Ward, Margaret, *Hanna Sheehy Skeffington - a Life*, Cork, 1997.
40. Ward, Margaret, *Unmanageable Revolutionaries*, London, 1983.

Newspapers

Irish News
Sligo Champion
Sligo Independent

Index